MW00397383

Silver Spoons
Blueberry Afternoons

A Crowning Collection of Recipes and Memories from
the National Association of Junior Auxiliaries, Inc.

Silver Spoons
Blueberry Afternoons

A Crowning Collection of Recipes and Memories from
the National Association of Junior Auxiliaries, Inc.

Published by the National Association of Junior Auxiliaries, Inc.

Copyright © 2008 by
National Association of Junior Auxiliaries, Inc.
P. O. Box 1873
Greenville, Mississippi 38702
www.najanet.org

Original Artwork: Mandy Buchanan, Active Member of the JA of Laurel, MS

This cookbook is a collection of favorite recipes, which are not necessarily original recipes, donated to the NAJA from its chapters and members for use in this book.

All rights reserved. No part of this publication may be reproduced in any form or by any means, electronic or mechanical, including photocopying and recording, or by any information storage or retrieval system, without prior written permission from the National Association of Junior Auxiliaries, Inc.

Library of Congress Control Number: 2007941947
ISBN: 978-0-9799789-0-6

Edited, Designed, and Produced by
Favorite Recipes® Press
An imprint of

FRP

P. O. Box 305142
Nashville, Tennessee 37230
800-358-0560

Art Director and Book Design: Starletta Polster
Project Editor: Mary Spotswood Box

Manufactured in the United States of America
First Printing: 2008
10,000 copies

Dedication

This book is dedicated to the chapters of the National Association of Junior Auxiliaries, Inc. Their selfless devotion to the principles of NAJA, to make a difference in the lives of those in need, particularly children, and their many contributions, including the recipes and stories in this book, truly make them the angels of NAJA.

Abbeville, LA

Amite, LA

Amory, MS

Arkadelphia, AR

Batesville, MS

Benton, AR

Biloxi-Ocean Springs, MS

Booneville, MS

Brookhaven, MS

Byram-Terry, MS

Cabot, AR

Camden, AR

Clarksdale, MS

Clarksville, AR

Clarksville, TN

Cleveland, MS

Cleveland, TN

Clinton, MS

Collierville, TN

Columbia, MS

Columbia, TN

Columbus, MS

Conway, AR

Corinth, MS

Covington-Tipton
County, TN

Crittenden County, AR

Crossett, AR

Crystal Springs, MS

DeSoto County, MS

East St. Mary, LA

Eastern Shore, AL

Eunice, LA

Forrest City, AR

Franklin, TN

Greenville, MS

Greenwood, MS

Grenada, MS

Gulfport, MS

Hammond, LA

Harrison, AR

Hattiesburg, MS

Hope, AR

Hot Springs, AR

Houma, LA

Humboldt, TN

Iberia Parish, LA

Independence
County, AR

Indianola, MS

Jackson County, AR

Jacksonville, AR

Jonesboro, AR

Kosciusko, MS

Lake Providence, LA

Laurel, MS

Lawrence County, TN

Leland, MS

Lewisburg, TN

Louisville, MS

Macon, MS

Madison County, FL

Madison-Ridgeland, MS

McComb, MS

McMinnville, TN

Meridian, MS

Milan, TN

Monticello, AR

Mountain Home, AR

Mt. Pleasant, TX

Nashville, AR

Natchez, MS

New Albany, MS

Obion County, TN

Osceola, AR

Oxford, MS

Paragould, AR

Pascagoula-Moss
Point, MS

Philadelphia, MS

Phillips County, AR

Picayune, MS

Rankin County, MS

Ripley-Lauderdale
County, TN

Rogers-Bentonville, AR

Russellville, AR

Ruston, LA

Savannah, TN

Scott County, MS

Searcy, AR

Slidell, LA

Starkville, MS

Taney County, MO

Tate-Panola County, MS

Tishomingo County, MS

Tupelo, MS

Vicksburg, MS

Warren, AR

Washington County, AR

Water Valley, MS

Wayne County, MS

West Point, MS

Winona, MS

Yazoo City, MS

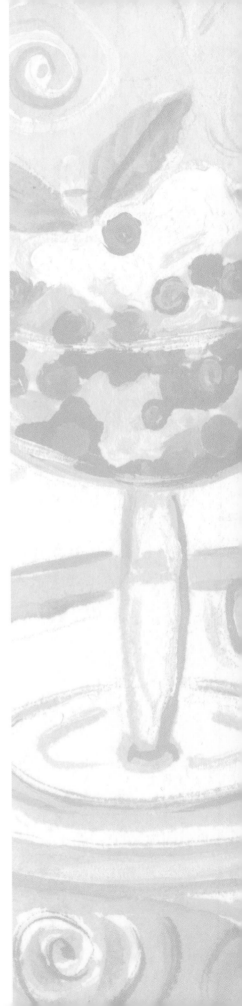

Table of Contents

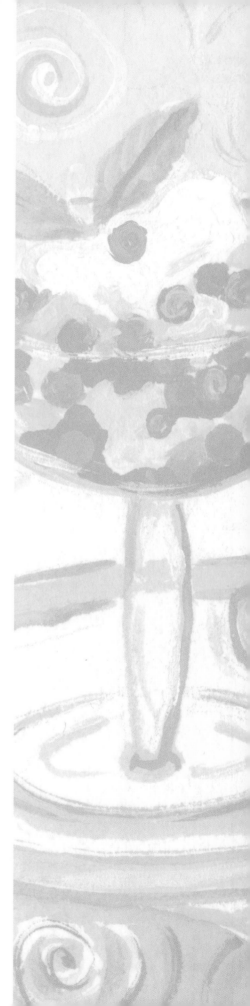

Mission Statement

To provide support, resources, and educational, leadership, cultural, and healthcare training for NAJA members in order to optimize community service by NAJA chapters.

"Care Today—Character Tomorrow"

JUNIOR AUXILIARY REPRESENTS A SERIOUS ENDEAVOR ON THE PART OF WOMEN TO BE ACTIVE AND CONSTRUCTIVE COMMUNITY PARTICIPANTS AND TO ASSUME LEADERSHIP ROLES IN MEETING COMMUNITY NEEDS. JUNIOR AUXILIARY PROVIDES THE MEMBER WITH THE OPPORTUNITY TO SERVE AND TO BE A VITAL PART OF THE COMMUNITY AND ENCOURAGES MEMBERS TO RENDER CHARITABLE SERVICES WHICH ARE BENEFICIAL TO THE GENERAL PUBLIC, WITH PARTICULAR EMPHASIS ON CHILDREN.

All proceeds from the sale of this book will be used to benefit NAJA, its chapters, and the families and children in the communities they serve.

Foreword

In 1985 and 1986, I had the honor of being president of the Junior Auxiliary of Russellville, Arkansas. It was my first opportunity to follow rules of business etiquette and protocol and to lead my peers. While I am sure I made many mistakes, the chapter members were gracious and dedicated, and together we achieved a terrific year *serving children* and *making a difference*. This great experience gave me confidence, encouragement, and lifelong friendships—and a leadership opportunity that was destined to be the foundation of my business style. Years later I started an international baking company, Tennessee Bun Company, leading over 250 employees to serve elite customers including McDonald's, Pepperidge Farms, and Chili's. I believe that in my brief year as president of my JA chapter, I learned so much more than Robert's Rules of Order and how to gain consensus. It was through my experience with Junior Auxiliary that I truly gained the courage to make a difference! In purchasing this cookbook, you will help support NAJA as they continue to train other young women—just as they helped me—to succeed in business as well as life, and to be constructive, productive, and dedicated members of their communities. Your contribution will help support JA chapters and the projects they undertake to better serve the needs of children and their families. THANK YOU for helping to make a difference!

Cordia Harrington

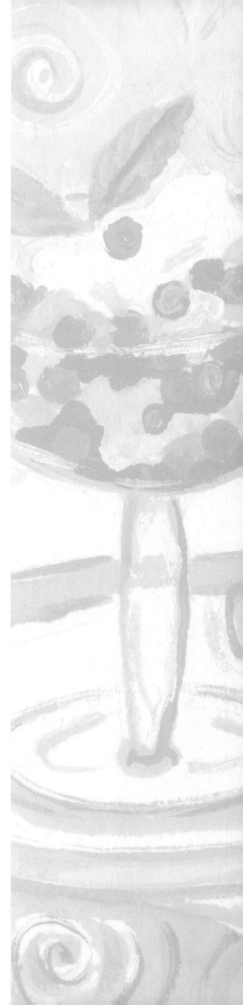

Families, Friends, Food

This premier edition of *Silver Spoons, Blueberry Afternoons*, presented by the National Association of Junior Auxiliaries, is a delightful collection of our recipes, our recollections, and our rewards, and it incorporates these three ingredients into the fabric of the work that has truly blessed an amazing number of lives through the years.

The Association was organized on November 3, 1941, when one hundred enthusiastic women from ten towns in Mississippi and Arkansas met in Greenville, Mississippi. Their goal was to unite the efforts of their local organizations in helping poverty-stricken families in their communities who had been devastated by the economic depression that began in the late 1920s. These families desperately needed food, clothing, and healthcare, primarily for their children.

World War II caused a shift for a time from care of children to home defense measures and war work. During the second year of this new organization's existence, members began to pool their food ration coupons to ensure that needy children would have adequate food to eat.

By the end of the war, the total membership had increased to 640. The services Junior Auxiliary provided for families had also increased. JA members were assigned to take care of individual families. This not only included food and clothing, but also taking care of their physical needs. (Many times I sat in the doctor's office with my mother and her sick JA children.) While we no longer assign each member a family, the love and care for children continues to be the main focus of Junior Auxiliary.

Today, many, many years later, Junior Auxiliary chapters cover the South and members continue the effort to expand our service area. Each local chapter promotes and enhances the National Association's legacy of volunteer service. By working together, the members of each chapter in the Association provide hope for our country's next generation. Today more than ever, children and families are in crisis . . . and Junior Auxiliary members are reaching out to them. Through workshops and seminars, volunteers learn about the latest issues affecting children and their families. They learn ways to address those issues and then take these ideas back to their chapters and communities. As the chapters work to identify specific needs within their own communities, they are then equipped to develop projects to meet them.

No organization could maintain such a remarkable program of community involvement without an equally amazing level of financial support. JA chapters earn support through fund-raising events that reflect the same standards of excellence that characterize their service projects.

In 1950 the National Association of Junior Auxiliaries adopted its permanent slogan, "Care Today—Character Tomorrow." Then, as now, JA volunteers shared a commitment to caring and to making a difference in the lives of children and their families. The value of Junior Auxiliary can be seen in the faces of those we touch . . . whose lives are truly changed for the better, thanks to an association of women who possess the passion and drive to make a difference. Bound by friendship and committed to selfless service, our members share a vision and a common purpose—to build a better tomorrow for the children on our doorstep today.

Families, friends, and food: we are thankful that families have been strengthened through Junior Auxiliary; that lifelong friendships have been made through Junior Auxiliary; and for the opportunity we have been given to provide the food that brings us all together.

May you enjoy.

Merrill Greenlee
Executive Director

The 101st Delegate

We knew we needed to set some rules and form a plan for all of us to follow. After all, some of those women from across the river would get it all wrong and it would be so tacky. Louise Eskrigge Crump from Greenville, Mississippi, who always liked to be in charge and give everyone orders, wrote all of us on both sides of the river she knew had been involved in community groups like the Junior Auxiliary of Greenville. We had been helping all of those poor children and their families since the Depression hit so hard. Louise had gotten the Greenville Country Club to allow us to meet there on November 3 for lunch. I worried all week about what hat to wear. I knew I would wear my good gray suit with black suede pumps and bag and my dove-gray gloves, but I could not decide if my black cloche with the pheasant feathers or the gray felt with the cartwheel brim was more stylish. I finally decided that morning on the cloche and thought I looked particularly chic as I drove the Packard into Greenville. I had to leave 2 1/2 hours early because of that dirt road leading to the new bridge going into town.

Hebe Crittenden had been in charge of arranging the chicken à la king on waffles luncheon and persuaded the kitchen staff to prepare her marvelous pickled peach congealed salad. After we all oohed and aahed over Margaret's new haircut she had just gotten in Memphis (a darling permanent wave with a swoop over her forehead), Louise told all of us to find a table and we would begin the meeting. Louise asked us to stand as a group and introduce ourselves from the towns we represented. There were one hundred of us there that afternoon from ten towns in Arkansas and Mississippi. After we took turns telling what we were doing for the poor at home, Louise, again, asked us if we thought forming a united club or something to set some rules and guidelines for all of us to follow would be a good idea. We all agreed. Louise already had a plan designed, however, to get us started and divided us into committees. We spent some time trying to decide when to meet again, and after it was determined that November 12 would not be good because Martha Ann Reese from Pine Bluff was having a sherry party for Bootsie Jamison née Walters, we agreed to meet for lunch again in the meeting room at the clinic in Greenville on November 14. I signed to be on the luncheon committee and agreed to bring Mama's Parker House rolls; those rolls are famous as the lightest little things anywhere on the river.

Recipes marked with this symbol throughout the book designate an NAJA chapter spotlight recipe.

We all came back on the 14th, and I wore my navy dress with the swing jacket and Grandmother's pearls. After a delicious luncheon including divine crab imperial from Vivian Elliott of Laurel, Mississippi, and precious pecan tassies from Ethlyn Wainwright of Russellville, Arkansas, we began our first official meeting. Louise said the first thing that needed to be done was to elect a president. Her good friend, Harriet Jefferts, immediately jumped up and nominated Louise. We all just rolled our eyes and said, "Aye." I do not think anyone was surprised. Louise just smiled and went right on as if she had just written all of those notes in her handbag. She called for committee reports and asked the constitution committee to distribute copies of what they had decided. They had evidently gotten a school somewhere to let them use a mimeograph machine because all of the copies were in purple ink. We had just finished reading the draft when we heard a titter in the back of the room. We turned around and watched as row after row stood up and skittered around, some climbing onto chairs. The next thing I knew, something ran across my foot, and I looked down to see a mouse scurrying under Lena's chair. I yelped and climbed onto my chair, too. Louise was banging on the table with a little brass hammer she just happened to have in her handbag. Someone in the back yelled, "I move to accept this constitution." We all screamed, "Yea," and about that time the mouse ran up to the head table, sat up on his haunches, and looked right at Louise. He must have recognized her because he began to shiver. Louise looked right back at him, grabbed her throat, and yelled, "This meeting is adjourned." She grabbed the papers in front of her and beat all of us out the back door.

And that is the story of how NAJA actually got started.

—Written with great liberties from the annals of NAJA history

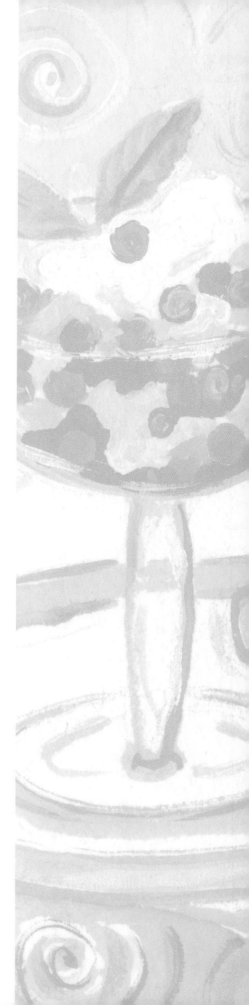

Appetizers & Beverages

The Courage to Support Us

Monday, August 8, 2005, President Susan Slaughter called the monthly meeting of the Junior Auxiliary of Hattiesburg to order. Enthusiasm was high for another busy JA year. Little did we know that in twenty-one days the worst natural disaster recorded in American history would make landfall just 60 miles south of our service area.

Monday, September 19, 2005, President Slaughter called the monthly meeting of the JAH to order. But this time, instead of enthusiasm, the room was filled with anxiety and tears. It was twenty-two days after the hurricane, and even the chapter itself was displaced—our regular meeting site was being used as a shelter. Susan read a letter from Lyn Patrick, NAJA President, that addressed the impact the disaster had on the chapters in the hurricane zone and announced that the area meeting in Slidell had been canceled—more evidence that life was on hold. ➤

Our board recommended that we cancel Charity Ball, our sole source for funding service projects. We agreed that our focus needed to be on meeting the immediate needs of our community as well as those brought our way by Katrina. Many Charity Ball auction items had been secured in the summer months, but the donors insisted we keep them. So we held an auction following our December meeting and invited past members to attend. Between the auction and monetary donations—and the generosity of our wonderful community—JAH still netted $92,000!

Thus, Charity Ball gave way to our "Hurricane Katrina Plan of Action," whereby we volunteered at Christian Services, local shelters, Catholic Social Services, hosted a blood drive, and worked at schools. Members were asked to devote at least eight hours to hurricane-related projects. Many of our members who were selflessly meeting the needs of others were in need themselves. Of seventy-two members surveyed, sixty-two received damage to their homes, some even having to relocate, twenty-four received business damage, twenty-one housed other displaced families, and most went weeks without power or running water.

Despite these circumstances, JAH members spent a total of 790 hours in hurricane-relief activities. The effects of Hurricane Katrina are still evident in our community today, but Junior Auxiliary of Hattiesburg never forgot its mission—to help others in their need. We did not use the devastating effects of Katrina as an excuse for a "light" year. We used Katrina as an opportunity to "do unto others as you would have them do unto you."

Romano and Prawn-Stuffed Mushrooms

1 pound freshwater prawns, peeled and deveined
Olive oil for sautéing
Salt or seasoning salt to taste
8 ounces cream cheese, softened
1/2 cup (2 ounces) grated Romano cheese
1 teaspoon Worcestershire sauce
1/4 teaspoon garlic powder
4 to 6 dashes of hot red pepper sauce
40 large mushrooms, stems removed
White wine
1/4 cup (1 ounce) grated Romano cheese

Sauté the prawns in a small amount of olive oil in a skillet for 2 to 3 minutes. Season with salt while cooking. Do not overcook. Let stand until cool. Chop the prawns into bite-size pieces. Mix the cream cheese, 1/2 cup Romano cheese, the Worcestershire sauce, garlic powder and hot sauce in a bowl; mix well. Stir in the prawns. Spoon into the mushroom caps. Place on a lightly greased baking sheet. Sprinkle with wine and 1/4 cup Romano cheese. Bake at 400 degrees for 15 to 20 minutes. These freeze well.

MAKES 40

Marinated Shrimp with Orange

3 pounds large shrimp, peeled and deveined
2 garlic cloves, crushed
1 1/2 cups apple cider vinegar
2/3 cup fresh lemon juice
1/2 cup ketchup
1/4 cup sugar
2 tablespoons minced parsley
2 teaspoons mustard seeds
1 teaspoon celery seeds
2 teaspoons salt
1/4 teaspoon pepper
1 cup vegetable oil
4 oranges, peeled and sectioned
4 white onions, thinly sliced
2 tablespoons drained capers

Cook the shrimp in boiling water in a large saucepan for 2 minutes or until the shrimp turn pink. Drain and rinse immediately with cold water to stop the cooking process. Mix the garlic, vinegar, lemon juice, ketchup, sugar, parsley, mustard seeds, celery seeds, salt and pepper in a large bowl. Add the oil gradually, whisking constantly until mixed well. Add the shrimp, orange sections, onions and capers. Toss until coated. Chill, covered, for 8 to 10 hours, stirring occasionally. Serve in scallop shells or in a large serving bowl with cocktail picks.

SERVES 6

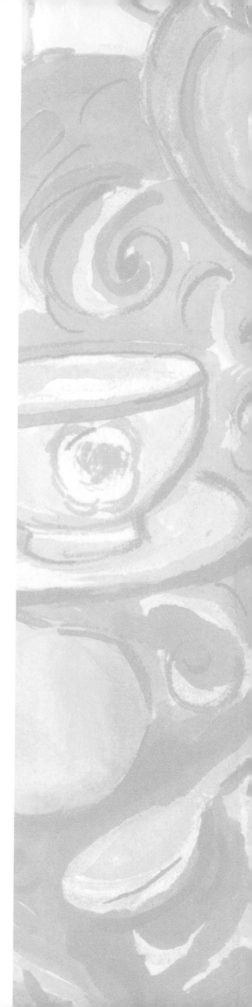

JA chapters are recognized for their extraordinary work throughout the year with the presentation of awards at the annual meeting. Among the most coveted awards are the Louise Eskrigge Crump Award for the most outstanding project satisfying the National Service Project guidelines, the Martha Wise Award for the most outstanding new project, the Norma DeLong Education Award for the most outstanding chapter education project, and the MAG Award for the most outstanding provisional class project.

Texas-Style Bacon-Wrapped Barbecue Shrimp

30 extra-large shrimp, peeled
  and butterflied
1/4 cup barbecue dry rub
5 jalapeño chiles or other hot chiles

15 slices bacon, cut into
  halves horizontally
2 lemons, cut into halves

Sprinkle each shrimp butterflied side up with 1/4 teaspoon of the dry rub. Slice the jalapeño chiles into 1/4-inch strips. Place one strip down the center of each shrimp. Close the shrimp. Wrap each shrimp lengthwise with one piece of the bacon. Squeeze two lemon halves over the bacon-wrapped shrimp just before cooking. Place on a lightly oiled grill rack. Grill over medium-hot coals with the hood closed for 3 minutes or until the bacon is crisp and brown. Turn the shrimp and squeeze the remaining lemon halves over the shrimp. Grill for 2 minutes or until the bacon is brown and the shrimp are pink. Serve immediately.

Makes 30

Crab-Stuffed Eggs

6 hard-cooked eggs
3 tablespoons chopped celery
1/4 cup (rounded) mayonnaise
1 teaspoon dry mustard
4 dashes of Worcestershire sauce
2 to 3 pinches of oregano

1/4 teaspoon parsley flakes
1/4 teaspoon salt
1 dash of Tabasco sauce
Pepper to taste
8 ounces crab meat

Slice the eggs into halves. Remove the yolks. Mix the egg yolks, celery, mayonnaise, dry mustard, Worcestershire sauce, oregano, parsley, salt, Tabasco sauce and pepper in a bowl. Fold in the crab meat. Spoon into the egg whites. Chill, covered, until serving time.

Makes 12

Pecan Catfish Paté

8 ounces cream cheese, softened
1 teaspoon horseradish
1 tablespoon lemon juice
1/4 teaspoon liquid smoke
1 teaspoon salt and pepper spice mix

4 (3- to 5-ounce) catfish fillets, poached and chopped
3 green onions, finely chopped
1 cup chopped pecans

Mix the cream cheese, horseradish, lemon juice, liquid smoke and spice mix in a bowl. Fold in the catfish and green onions. Chill, covered, for 3 to 4 hours. Shape into a ball. Roll in the pecans. Serve at room temperature with wheat crackers. This recipe may be doubled and it freezes well.

SERVES 8

Swedish Meatballs with Zesty Apricot Sauce

MAIN STREET, *the cookbook of the Junior Auxiliary of Franklin, Tennessee, includes this recipe. The JA of Franklin furnishes new winter coats to needy children through the* COAT OF MANY COLORS *project.*

MEATBALLS
2 slices bread
2 pounds ground beef
1 1/2 envelopes onion soup mix

ZESTY APRICOT SAUCE
1 cup ketchup
1 cup apricot nectar
8 teaspoons apple cider vinegar
8 teaspoons brown sugar
4 teaspoons horseradish
2 teaspoons Worcestershire sauce

To prepare the meatballs, sprinkle the bread with water until completely moistened. Squeeze out any excess water. Mix the bread, ground beef and soup mix in a large bowl. Shape into small balls and place in a shallow baking pan sprayed with nonstick cooking spray. Bake at 350 degrees for 20 minutes or until cooked through, turning occasionally; drain.

To prepare the sauce, combine the ketchup, apricot nectar, vinegar, brown sugar, horseradish and Worcestershire sauce in a large saucepan. Bring to a simmer, stirring frequently. Simmer for 10 minutes. Add the meatballs and simmer until heated through. The meatballs may be frozen before cooking.

MAKES 3 TO 4 DOZEN

Salsa Cheesecake

ANGEL TREE

In October, teachers nominate K–5 students in the community for our project. We interview parents to determine needs and wishes. Trees with ornaments containing this information are placed in area businesses for the community to adopt. Patrons buy and wrap the gifts. JA members deliver gifts to incredibly grateful parents, who know their children will now have Christmas. It's what JA is all about.

—JA OF WARREN

16 ounces cream cheese, softened
2 cups (8 ounces) shredded Monterey Jack cheese or Colby-Monterey Jack cheese blend
1 cup sour cream
3 eggs
1 cup mild or hot salsa
1 (4-ounce) can diced green chiles, drained
1 cup sour cream
1 (6-ounce) container frozen avocado dip or guacamole, thawed
1 tomato, peeled, seeded and chopped

Beat the cream cheese in a mixing bowl until light and fluffy. Add the Monterey Jack cheese and 1 cup sour cream. Beat until combined. Add the eggs and beat at low speed just until combined. Stir in the salsa and green chiles.

Press heavy-duty foil tightly over the bottom and up the side of a 9-inch springform pan to prevent leaking. Spoon the cream cheese mixture in the pan. Set the pan in a larger shallow pan. Add hot water to the larger pan to come halfway up the side of the springform pan. Bake at 350 degrees for 35 to 40 minutes or until the center is almost set. Remove to a wire rack.

Spoon 1 cup sour cream onto the top of the hot cheesecake. Let stand for 1 minute. Spread the sour cream evenly over the top. Let stand until cool. Chill, covered, for 4 to 24 hours.

To serve, run a sharp knife around the edge of the cheesecake and remove the side of the pan. Spoon the avocado dip around the top outside edge. Sprinkle with the tomato. Garnish with snipped fresh cilantro or parsley. Serve with tortilla chips, melba toasts or crackers. Additional chopped avocado may be stirred into the avocado dip, if desired.

SERVES 20

Berry Pecan Cheese Ring

This recipe is from the Junior Auxiliary of Warren, Arkansas. The JA of Warren provides books three times a year to area schoolchildren in kindergarten through sixth grade.

16 ounces extra-sharp Cheddar
   cheese, shredded
16 ounces Cheddar cheese,
   shredded
1 cup mayonnaise
1 teaspoon cayenne pepper

1 bunch green onions,
   finely chopped
1 cup pecans
1 jar strawberry preserves or
   raspberry preserves

Mix the extra-sharp Cheddar cheese, Cheddar cheese, mayonnaise, cayenne pepper and green onions in a bowl. Sprinkle 1/4 cup of the pecans in the bottom of a plastic wrap-lined tube pan or mold. Press the cheese mixture into the pan. Chill, covered, for 8 to 10 hours. Invert onto a serving platter and remove the plastic wrap. Press the remaining 3/4 cup pecans over the outside. Spoon the preserves into the center of the cheese ring. Serve with crackers.

SERVES 12

Pesto Cream Cheese Ball

16 ounces cream cheese, softened
4 ounces pesto
1/2 cup sun-dried tomatoes, sliced

1/2 cup capers
1/2 cup chopped green onions
1/2 cup pine nuts

Beat the cream cheese and pesto in a mixing bowl until combined. Shape into a ball. Roll in a mixture of the sun-dried tomatoes, capers, green onions and pine nuts. Serve with crackers. May layer the cream cheese mixture and tomato mixture in a serving dish instead of shaping into a ball.

SERVES 12

Buffalo Chicken Dip

This recipe is from the Junior Auxiliary of Macon, Mississippi. The JA of Macon volunteers at a camp for terminally ill children in the CAMP RISING SUN *project.*

16 ounces cream cheese, chopped
2 (6-ounce) packages white meat chicken, or 2 chicken breasts, boiled and chopped

1 cup ranch salad dressing
5 ounces buffalo wing sauce
2 cups (8 ounces) shredded sharp Cheddar cheese

Melt the cream cheese in a skillet, stirring frequently. Stir in the chicken, salad dressing, and buffalo wing sauce. Pour into a baking dish. Sprinkle with the Cheddar cheese. Bake at 350 degrees for 20 to 30 minutes. Serve with celery sticks or corn chips.

MAKES 3 TO 4 CUPS

Hot Chicken Dip

The Junior Auxiliary of Lake Providence, Louisiana, submitted this recipe. The JA of Lake Providence won the 2005 Martha Wise Award for their CLASSROOM CLEAN-UP *project.*

1 (10-ounce) can cream of chicken soup
16 ounces cream cheese, softened
1 cup mayonnaise
2 (12-ounce) cans chicken
1 bunch green onions, chopped

Cayenne pepper to taste
Garlic powder to taste
Onion powder to taste
2 cups (8 ounces) shredded taco cheese blend

Mix the soup, cream cheese and mayonnaise in a bowl. Stir in the chicken and green onions. Season with cayenne pepper, garlic powder and onion powder. Spoon into a baking dish and sprinkle with the taco cheese blend. Bake at 350 degrees until bubbly. Serve with chips.

MAKES 6 TO 8 CUPS

Baked Ham and Cheddar Cheese Dip

2 cups (8 ounces) shredded sharp
   Cheddar cheese, softened
1 (4-ounce) can chopped
   green chiles

1 cup chopped smoked ham
16 ounces cream cheese, softened
1 cup sour cream

Mix the Cheddar cheese, green chiles, ham, cream cheese and sour cream in a bowl. Spoon into a baking dish. Bake at 350 degrees for 20 to 30 minutes or until bubbly. Serve with butter crackers.

SERVES 32

Hot Crab and Jalapeño Chile Dip

8 ounces crab meat
$1/2$ red bell pepper, chopped
$1^1/2$ teaspoons olive oil
1 (14-ounce) can artichoke hearts,
   drained and chopped
1 cup mayonnaise
$1/2$ cup (2 ounces) freshly grated
   Parmesan cheese

$1/4$ cup thinly sliced green onions
1 tablespoon Worcestershire sauce
1 tablespoon finely chopped
   pickled jalapeño chile
$1^1/2$ teaspoons fresh lemon juice
$1/2$ teaspoon celery salt
Salt and pepper to taste
$1/3$ cup slivered almonds

Drain and gently pick through the crab meat, discarding any bits of shell or cartilage; set aside. Sauté the bell pepper in the hot olive oil in a skillet for 3 minutes or until tender. Remove to a large bowl. Add the artichoke hearts, mayonnaise, cheese, green onions, Worcestershire sauce, jalapeño chile, lemon juice and celery salt; mix well. Fold in the crab meat. Season with salt and pepper. Spread in an 8-inch quiche pan or a pie plate with a $1^1/2$-inch-high side. Sprinkle with the almonds. Bake at 375 degrees for 30 minutes or until light brown and bubbly. Serve warm.

MAKES 3 TO 4 CUPS

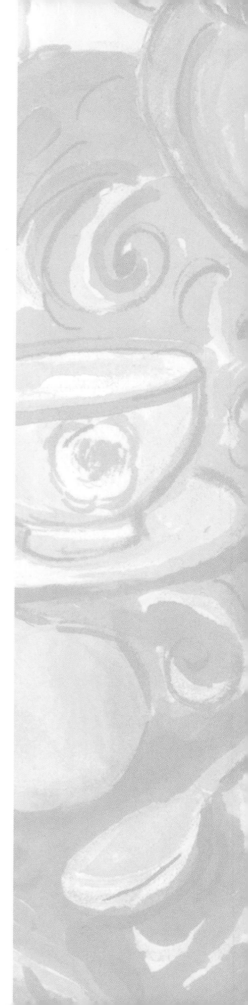

Jalapeño Chile Dip

The Junior Auxiliary of Mount Pleasant, Texas, selected this recipe as a favorite. The JA of Mount Pleasant hosts a Christmas party for underprivileged children with the BREAKFAST WITH SANTA *project.*

2 cups (8 ounces) shredded sharp
    Cheddar cheese or extra-sharp
    Cheddar cheese
2 cups chopped pecans

$1^3/4$ cups mayonnaise
$1^1/4$ cups chopped green onions
1 (6-ounce) jar red or green
    jalapeño chile jelly

Mix the cheese, pecans, mayonnaise and green onions in a bowl. Spoon onto a serving dish or into a serving bowl. Spread the jelly over the top. Serve with crackers.

SERVES 8 TO 10

Baked Pimento Cheese Dip

8 ounces extra-sharp Cheddar
    cheese, shredded
8 ounces sharp Cheddar
    cheese, shredded
1 small onion, chopped

1 (4-ounce) jar pimentos, drained
$1^1/2$ cups mayonnaise
1 teaspoon Worcestershire sauce
$1/4$ teaspoon cayenne pepper

Mix the extra-sharp Cheddar cheese, Cheddar cheese, onion, pimentos, mayonnaise, Worcestershire sauce and cayenne pepper in a large bowl. Spoon into a lightly greased 3-quart baking dish. Bake at 350 degrees for 20 minutes. Serve hot with butter crackers or other crackers.

MAKES 8 TO 10

She handed me the baby and ran over to the rack of coats. The baby, diaper dirty, nose running, and drooling on my shirt, continued to sleep. I walked and rocked until, an hour later, she came back with coats for all her family under her arm. "This is the first time since he was born that anyone, other than me, has held him so I could do something alone."

—COATS FOR KIDS

Baked Vidalia Onion Dip

3 large Vidalia onions, chopped
2 tablespoons butter or margarine
2 cups (8 ounces) shredded
   Swiss cheese
1 garlic clove, minced

1 (8-ounce) can water chestnuts,
   drained and chopped (optional)
1/4 cup dry white wine
1/2 teaspoon hot red pepper sauce

Sauté the onions in the butter in a large skillet over medium-high heat for
10 minutes or until tender. Mix the cheese, garlic, water chestnuts, wine and hot
sauce in a bowl. Stir into the onions. Spoon into a lightly greased 2-quart baking
dish. Bake at 350 degrees for 25 minutes or until golden brown. Let stand for
10 minutes. Serve with crackers or tortilla chips.

SERVES 32

Spinach Artichoke Dip

*This recipe is from the Junior Auxiliary of Humboldt, Tennessee. The JA
of Humboldt's project,* OPERATION KIDPRINT, *provides and helps complete
identification cards for children to include in their family records.*

1/4 cup (1/2 stick) butter
1/4 cup all-purpose flour
1/4 cup chopped onion
1 teaspoon vegetable oil
1/4 teaspoon cayenne pepper
1/4 teaspoon garlic powder
3/4 cup chicken broth
1 quart cream, or 1 pint cream plus
   1 pint half-and-half

2 ounces Romano cheese, grated
12 ounces American cheese, sliced
Salt and black pepper to taste
1 1/2 cups canned artichokes
1 pound chopped spinach
8 slices Swiss cheese

Melt the butter in a saucepan. Stir in the flour. Cook over medium-low heat
until smooth and thickened, stirring constantly. Sauté the onion in the oil in a
large skillet until tender. Stir in the cayenne pepper, garlic powder and broth.
Bring to a boil. Reduce the heat and simmer until reduced by one-half. Add the
cream gradually, stirring constantly until blended. Stir in the Romano cheese
and American cheese. Season with salt and black pepper. Add the flour mixture
gradually, stirring constantly until smooth. Add the artichokes and spinach.
Simmer until slightly thickened, stirring constantly. Pour into a baking dish.
Top with the Swiss cheese. Bake at 400 degrees until bubbly. Serve with tortilla
chips. This dip freezes well.

MAKES 2 QUARTS

AWARD WINNER:
HOST THE COAST—
JA OF SCOTT COUNTY
*During the recovery from
Hurricane Katrina, our
chapter members worked
with local community
members and organized
"Host the Coast." As a
chapter, we decided to
reach beyond our normal
service area to assist a JA
chapter directly affected
by the hurricane.*

Black-Eyed Pea Salsa

1 (16-ounce) can black-eyed peas
2 tomatoes, chopped
1 bunch green onions, chopped
1 or 2 garlic cloves, minced
1 tablespoon chopped fresh cilantro

3 tablespoons fresh lime juice
1 tablespoon olive oil
1/2 teaspoon cumin
1/4 teaspoon salt

Rinse and drain the black-eyed peas in a colander. Mix the tomatoes, green onions, garlic, cilantro, lime juice, olive oil, cumin and salt in a bowl. Fold in the black-eyed peas. Chill, covered, for 4 hours. Serve with tortilla chips.

MAKES 4 CUPS

Corn and Mango Salsa

5 garlic cloves, minced
2 tablespoons water
2 tablespoons sugar
1 1/2 teaspoons salt
1 teaspoon chili powder
3/4 teaspoon cumin
1/2 teaspoon oregano
1/2 teaspoon cayenne pepper
1/2 teaspoon black pepper
1/3 cup lime juice (about 2 limes)
1/2 cup vegetable oil

8 ears white corn
Salt to taste
2 mangoes, chopped
2 tomatoes, seeded and chopped
1 red onion, finely chopped
1 bunch green onions, thinly sliced
2 jalapeño chiles, finely chopped,
   or more to taste
1/2 cup minced cilantro
2 avocados

Mix the garlic, water, sugar, 1 1/2 teaspoons salt, chili powder, cumin, oregano, cayenne pepper and black pepper in a bowl. Whisk in the lime juice and oil. Boil the corn in lightly salted water in a saucepan for 10 to 15 minutes or until tender. Drain and rinse with cold water or place in an ice water bath to stop the cooking process; drain. Cut the kernels from the cobs and place in a large bowl. Discard the cobs. Add the mangoes, tomatoes, red onion, green onions, jalapeño chiles and cilantro; mix well. Whisk the dressing and pour over the corn mixture. Toss until coated. Chill, covered, for 4 to 10 hours. Peel, chop and fold in the avocados just before serving.

MAKES 6 CUPS

Almond Snack Mix

This is a favorite recipe of the members of the Junior Auxiliary of Taney County, Missouri. The S.I.P. Project, conducted by the JA of Taney County, collects and distributes nutritious weekend snacks to needy children in the community.

6 cups rice squares cereal
2 cups chopped almonds
1/2 cup sugar
1/2 cup light corn syrup

1/4 cup (1/2 stick) butter, chopped
1/4 teaspoon baking soda
1 1/2 teaspoons almond extract

Combine the cereal and almonds in a large mixing bowl. Combine the sugar, corn syrup and butter in a saucepan. Bring to a boil, stirring frequently. Remove from the heat and stir in the baking soda and almond extract. Pour over the cereal mixture and stir until coated. Spread out on a large baking sheet lined with foil. Bake at 250 degrees for 20 minutes. Stir the mixture. Bake for 20 minutes longer or until golden brown. Store in an airtight container.

MAKES 8 CUPS

Cayenne Pepper Cheese Straws

The Junior Auxiliary of Clinton, Mississippi, includes this recipe in the cookbook LET'S GET TOGETHER. *The JA of Clinton received the 2007 Martha Wise Award for* JA JUMPSTART, *a two-week camp to introduce children to school for the first time.*

8 ounces sharp Cheddar cheese or
extra-sharp Cheddar cheese,
freshly shredded
1/2 cup (1 stick) margarine, softened

1 cup (heaping) self-rising flour
3/4 teaspoon seasoned salt
1/2 teaspoon cayenne pepper

Combine the cheese, margarine, flour, seasoned salt and cayenne pepper in a bowl. Knead for 4 to 5 minutes or until the mixture forms a ball. Place the dough in a cookie press fitted with a star tip. Press finger-length pieces in rows approximately 1/4 inch apart onto two baking sheets sprayed with nonstick cooking spray. Bake at 325 degrees for 8 to 10 minutes or until golden brown on the bottom. Remove to paper towels and let stand to cool for 10 minutes. Store in sealable plastic bags inside tins.

MAKES ABOUT 6 DOZEN

"Our Charity Ball is the sole fund-raiser and a much-anticipated annual event for the Greenville chapter since 1950. Much of the excitement is the coronation of a King and Queen, chosen according to their community service and involvement, and kept secret until the night of the ball. The event kicks off with the Patrons' Party, a marvelous dinner buffet, and is followed by the coronation ceremony. Biographies are read as the royal couple makes their entrance, along with their court—kindergarten, 3rd, 8th, and 12th grade children of Associate/Life JA members. The royal couple has the first dance—and the party begins."

—ACTIVE MEMBER,
JA OF GREENVILLE

Pimento Cheese and Pineapple Sandwiches

2 cups (8 ounces) shredded sharp Cheddar cheese
1/2 cup mayonnaise
1 (4-ounce) jar sliced pimentos, drained
1 teaspoon fresh lemon juice
1/2 teaspoon finely chopped jalapeño chile (optional)

1/2 teaspoon grated sweet onion
1/2 teaspoon hot red pepper sauce
1/2 teaspoon Worcestershire sauce
1/2 teaspoon freshly ground pepper
Canned pineapple slices in pineapple juice, drained
Sliced white bread

Mix the cheese, mayonnaise, pimentos, lemon juice, jalapeño chile, onion, hot sauce, Worcestershire sauce and pepper in a bowl. Chill, covered, for 2 hours. Spread on 4 to 6 slices of bread. Top each with a slice of pineapple and a slice of bread. Trim and discard the crusts. Cut each sandwich into halves. These sandwiches will become soggy if prepared too far in advance.

MAKES 4 TO 6 SANDWICHES

Artichoke Bread

This recipe was submitted by the Junior Auxiliary of Greenville, Mississippi. The JA of Greenville is a charter chapter of NAJA, a member since 1941.

2 or 3 garlic cloves
2 teaspoons sesame seeds
1/4 cup (1/2 stick) butter
1 (14-ounce) can artichoke hearts, drained and chopped
1 cup (4 ounces) shredded Monterey Jack cheese

1 cup (4 ounces) grated Parmesan cheese
1/2 cup sour cream
1 loaf French bread
1/2 cup (2 ounces) shredded Cheddar cheese

Cook the garlic and sesame seeds in the butter in a skillet over medium-high heat until light brown, stirring constantly. Remove from the heat and stir in the artichoke hearts, Monterey Jack cheese, Parmesan cheese and sour cream. Cut the bread into halves lengthwise. Hollow out each half, leaving a 1-inch shell. Chop the bread and add to the artichoke mixture; mix well. Spoon into the bread shells and sprinkle with the Cheddar cheese. Place crust side down on a baking sheet and cover with foil. Bake at 350 degrees for 25 minutes. Bake, uncovered, for 5 minutes or until the cheese melts. Cut into bite-size pieces and serve hot.

SERVES 10 TO 12

Hot Cheese Loaf

1 large round sweet bread loaf
2 cups (8 ounces) shredded sharp
   Cheddar cheese
1 1/2 cups sour cream
1 tablespoon Worcestershire sauce

1 (2-ounce) jar dried chipped beef
1 (4-ounce) can diced green chiles
1 (2-ounce) jar pimento, drained
   and chopped

Slice off the top of the bread and scoop out the center. Tear the bread into bite-size pieces and set aside. Mix the cheese, sour cream, Worcestershire sauce, chipped beef, green chiles and pimento in a bowl. Spoon into the center of the bread. Wrap in foil and place on a baking sheet. Bake at 325 degrees for 1 1/2 hours. Serve with the bread pieces for dipping.

Serves 8 to 10

Southwestern Snack Squares

1 1/4 cups all-purpose flour
1 cup thinly sliced green onions
3/4 cup cornmeal
1 tablespoon brown sugar
2 teaspoons baking powder
1 teaspoon oregano
1/2 teaspoon cumin
1/4 teaspoon salt
1 cup milk
1/4 cup vegetable oil

1 egg
1 cup (4 ounces) shredded
   Cheddar cheese
1 (4-ounce) can chopped green
   chiles, drained
1/4 cup finely chopped red
   bell pepper
2 slices bacon, crisp-cooked and
   crumbled

Mix the flour, green onions, cornmeal, brown sugar, baking powder, oregano, cumin and salt in a large bowl. Mix the milk, oil and egg in a small bowl until smooth. Add to the cornmeal mixture and mix until just moistened. Spread in a greased 7×11-inch baking dish. Combine the cheese, green chiles, bell pepper and bacon in a bowl; mix well. Sprinkle over the top. Bake at 400 degrees for 25 to 30 minutes or until a wooden pick inserted in the center comes out clean. Let cool in the pan for 10 minutes.

Makes about 15 squares

Our chapter provides
necessities for needy children
in area schools. One year,
a counselor called requesting
a pair of shoes for a child
whose own shoes were so
badly worn they were
unable to determine the
size. A JA member asked her
to measure his feet with a
ruler. She went to Wal-Mart
with a ruler to measure
shoes until she was able to
find the correct size. The
shoes fit perfectly.

—JA OF JACKSONVILLE

Banana Punch

The Junior Auxiliary of Ripley-Lauderdale County, Tennessee, chose this recipe as a favorite. The JA of Ripley-Lauderdale County provides eye exams and glasses for needy children in the community.

4 cups sugar	1 (6-ounce) can frozen orange juice
6 cups water	concentrate, thawed
8 very ripe bananas	1 (16-ounce) jar maraschino cherries
Juice of 3 lemons	2 (1-quart) bottles ginger ale
1 (14-ounce) can pineapple juice	

Combine the sugar and water in a large saucepan. Bring to a boil, stirring frequently. Boil for 3 minutes. Let stand until cool. Mash the bananas in a bowl. Add the lemon juice immediately and mix well. Stir in the pineapple juice and orange juice concentrate. Drain the cherries, reserving the juice. Chop the cherries. Add the cherries, cherry juice and sugar syrup to the banana mixture; mix well.

Freeze in a freezer-safe container until ready to use. Thaw overnight in the refrigerator before serving. Combine the banana mixture and ginger ale in a punch bowl; mix well. The banana mixture can be frozen for up to 6 months.

MAKES ABOUT 20 CUPS

Tangy Punch

The Junior Auxiliary of Byram-Terry, Mississippi, contributed this recipe from the cookbook JA OF BYRAM-TERRY COOKBOOK. *The JA of Byram-Terry's* BEARS FOR YOU *project furnishes teddy bears to the local fire department to give to children involved in the tragedy of a fire.*

2¹/2 cups orange breakfast drink mix	1 (6-ounce) can frozen lemonade concentrate, thawed
3 quarts water	Ice
2 (46-ounce) cans pineapple juice	2 (2-liter) bottles lemon-lime soda

Mix the drink mix and water in a large container. Stir until dissolved. Stir in the pineapple juice and lemonade concentrate. Chill until cold. Pour over ice in a punch bowl. Stir in the lemon-lime soda.

SERVES 50

Anytime Punch

This recipe was submitted by the Junior Auxiliary of Jacksonville, Arkansas. The JA of Jacksonville keeps a street clean in the community with their Adopt-A-Street *project.*

2 quarts white grape juice, chilled
2 quarts ginger ale, chilled

1/2 gallon lime sherbet or
  other sherbet

Mix the grape juice and ginger ale in a punch bowl. Scoop the sherbet into cups and carefully ladle the punch over the sherbet. May place the scoops directly into the punch bowl instead.

Serves 20

Raspberry Tea Punch

1 quart water
4 tea bags
4 raspberry-flavored tea bags
1 1/4 cups sugar

1 (6-ounce) can frozen lemonade
  concentrate, thawed
1 (6-ounce) can frozen orange juice
  concentrate, thawed

Bring 1 quart water to a boil in a large saucepan. Remove from the heat and add the tea bags. Let steep for 15 to 20 minutes. Discard the tea bags. Add the sugar and stir until dissolved. Pour into a 1-gallon pitcher. Stir in the lemonade concentrate and orange juice concentrate. Fill the pitcher with additional water to make 1 gallon; chill until cold.

Makes 1 gallon

Springtime Punch

This recipe is from the Junior Auxiliary of Natchez, Mississippi. The JA of Natchez won the 2006 Louise Eskrigge Crump Award for Project Guardian Angel, *a project to provide the necessities to families of deployed National Guardsmen.*

1 (46-ounce) can pineapple juice
1 (64-ounce) jar apple juice

1 (2-liter) lemon-lime soda

Mix the pineapple juice, apple juice and lemon-lime soda in a large punch bowl. Serve over ice.

Serves 20

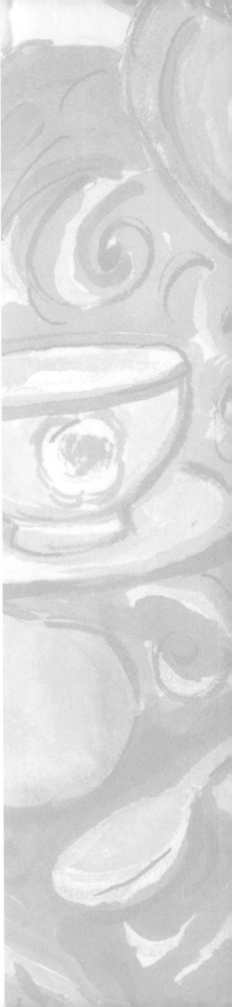

AWARD WINNER:

JUNIORS IN SERVICE—

JA OF SLIDELL

Juniors in Service (JIS) is a fund-raising project for Junior Auxiliary of Slidell whereby contributors make a $50 donation to JA in the name of a local high school junior. The program is designed to teach the sponsored students to identify areas of need in their community and requires them to volunteer twelve hours of their time toward community service. The objective is to encourage the act of voluntarism at a young age so that the Slidell community will benefit from these young adults in years to come.

NAJA Fiftieth Anniversary Punch

4 to 5 cups sugar
1/4 cup citric acid (optional)
2 quarts boiling water
1 (46-ounce) can unsweetened pineapple juice

1 (12-ounce) can frozen pink lemonade concentrate, thawed
1 (10-ounce) can frozen strawberry daiquiri mix, thawed
4 quarts water
8 (10-ounce) bottles ginger ale

Dissolve the sugar and citric acid in the boiling water in a large heatproof ceramic bowl. Stir in the pineapple juice, lemonade concentrate, daiquiri mix and 4 quarts water. Divide evenly among four 1-gallon sealable plastic freezer bags; freeze. Let stand at room temperature for 30 minutes before serving. Empty into a large punch bowl and break into chunks. Add the ginger ale and stir until slushy.

MAKES 2 1/2 GALLONS

Junior Auxiliary Punch

VINTAGE VICKSBURG, *the cookbook of the Junior Auxiliary of Vicksburg, Mississippi, contains this recipe. The JA of Vicksburg is a charter chapter of NAJA, a member since 1941.*

1/2 cup sugar
1/2 cup fresh lemon juice
2 fifths of sauterne

1 fifth of Champagne
1/2 cup brandy

Combine the sugar and lemon juice in a heatproof bowl. Stir until the sugar dissolves, heating the lemon juice if needed. Pour into a punch bowl. Add the sauterne, Champagne and brandy; mix well. Chill or serve with an ice ring.

SERVES 24

Christmas Punch

2 large grapefruit
1/2 (750-milliliter) bottle
   dry Champagne

Juice of 4 oranges
3 tablespoons sugar
10 to 12 fresh mint sprigs, snipped

Cut the grapefruit into halves lengthwise. Juice three halves and pour into a small punch bowl. Add the Champagne, orange juice, sugar and mint; mix well. Peel and section the remaining grapefruit half. Add to the punch bowl or punch cups. Serve immediately.

MAKES 4 CUPS

Holiday Nog

2 (1/2-gallon) containers vanilla ice
   cream, softened

1/2 (750-milliliter) bottle brandy
1/2 (750-milliliter) bottle Kahlúa

Place the ice cream in a large punch bowl. Pour the brandy and Kahlúa over the top. Stir until blended. Ladle into punch cups.

SERVES 20

Bourbon Slush

The Junior Auxiliary of Slidell, Louisiana, submitted this recipe from the chapter's cookbook, COOKING UP A STORM. *The* K BAR B BUDDY BRIGADE *project of the JAS provides one-on-one mentoring and emotional support for girls at a local youth ranch.*

2 cups water
4 tea bags
1 3/4 cups sugar
1 (12-ounce) can frozen lemonade
   concentrate, thawed

1 (12-ounce) can frozen orange
   juice concentrate, thawed
7 cups water
2 cups bourbon

Bring 2 cups water to a boil in a saucepan. Add the tea bags. Steep for 3 minutes. Discard the tea bags. Mix the sugar, lemonade concentrate and orange juice concentrate in a 5-quart freezer-safe container. Add the tea, 7 cups water and the bourbon; mix well. Freeze until the mixture becomes slushy, stirring occasionally.

MAKES 14 CUPS

Watermelon Slushy

2 cups chopped watermelon
1 1/2 cups ginger ale, half frozen

Pulse the watermelon in a food processor three or four times or until slightly chunky. Add the ginger ale and pulse for 1 second. Spoon into attractive glasses. Garnish with lime wedges.

SERVES 4

Fabulous Frozen Margaritas

2 fifths of tequila
1 pint Triple Sec
3 1/2 quarts water
1 cup lime juice

1/2 cup lemon juice
8 (6-ounce) cans frozen lemonade
    concentrate, thawed

Mix the tequila, Triple Sec, water, lime juice, lemon juice and lemonade concentrate in a freezer-safe container. Freeze for 36 hours. Serve in glasses rimmed with margarita salt, if desired.

SERVES 20

Mint Juleps

1 cup sugar
1 cup water
1 large handful fresh mint, torn
    into medium-size pieces

Crushed ice
16 ounces bourbon

Combine the sugar, water and mint in a saucepan and bring to a boil, stirring occasionally. Boil for 3 to 5 minutes or until the sugar has dissolved and the mint is wilted. Remove from the heat and let stand for 1 to 2 minutes or until slightly cool. Fill silver mint julep cups or medium-size drinking glasses with crushed ice. Pour 1 1/2 tablespoons of the sugar syrup and 2 ounces of the bourbon over the ice in each glass. Stir gently. Fill with additional crushed ice. Garnish each cup with a sprig of fresh mint.

SERVES 8

REGIONAL MEETINGS
"In 1982, NAJA voted not to reimburse expenses for national officers—a sign of the times. So, we scheduled all Regional Meetings back to back, traveling together and sleeping four to a room. We accomplished great things, but by the last week, we all looked pretty grim. I remember that Cindy and Ella Lea alternated wearing the same dress as a joke— and to this day, I still don't remember to whom the dress actually belonged!"

—ANN GUICE,
NAJA PRESIDENT, 1981–1982

Pomegranate Cosmopolitan

2/3 cup pomegranate juice
1/2 cup vodka
1/4 cup Cointreau or Triple Sec

2 teaspoons fresh lime juice
Ice

Combine the pomegranate juice, vodka, Cointreau and lime juice in a large cocktail shaker. Fill with ice. Shake vigorously and strain into two martini glasses. Garnish each glass with a lime twist.

MAKES 2

Ruby Relaxer

This recipe is a favorite of the Junior Auxiliary of Amite, Louisiana. The JA of Amite coordinates efforts to maintain a community playground through the PLAYGROUND PROJECT.

3 tablespoons each vodka, peach schnapps and coconut rum

3 tablespoons cranberry juice
1 cup pineapple juice

Mix all the ingredients in a pitcher; chill. Serve over ice in glasses.

SERVES 2

White Wine Sangria

The Junior Auxiliary of Picayune, Mississippi, submitted this recipe from the chapter's cookbook, A TASTE OF SOUTHERN CHARM. *The JAP screens schoolchildren for scoliosis each year with the* SCOLIOSIS PROJECT.

1 lemon, sliced, end pieces reserved
1 lime, sliced, end pieces reserved
2 oranges, sliced, end pieces reserved
1/2 cup sugar
1/2 cup water

1 pineapple section
1 quart chablis
1 cup sparkling mineral water
2 ounces Triple Sec
Crushed ice

Bring the end pieces of the fruits, sugar and water to a boil in a saucepan, stirring occasionally. Boil for 3 minutes. Remove from the heat and let stand until cool. Discard the end pieces. Mix the sugar syrup, pineapple, chablis, mineral water, Triple Sec, sliced fruit and ice in a large pitcher or punch bowl. Serve immediately.

SERVES 6

Brunch & Breads

The National Service Project

Since 1941 the primary emphasis of NAJA has been service to the community, and the major focus of that service has been improving the welfare of children. Every chapter in the Association is required to have at least one project each year to identify one at-risk child or children and provide food, clothing, shelter, and/or emotional support in an ongoing, personal relationship in order to break the cycle of dependency. ➤

This requirement is the single specific project duty that every chapter must include in their program of service annually. The welfare of children is the National Service Project of the Association. Because of this obligation, NAJA ensures that more than one hundred children each year are given encouragement, support, and direction to guarantee that they will become productive, successful adults. Many chapters work to sustain these at-risk children from childhood until they enter college and become flourishing adults. While working one-on-one regularly with these children, JA workers change lives, futures, and destinies with their direct, hands-on care and love.

Peaches and Cream-Stuffed French Toast

2 to 3 peaches, or 1 (16-ounce) can
   peach halves, drained
3 eggs
2 cups half-and-half
1/2 cup sugar
1 teaspoon vanilla extract
8 ounces cream cheese, softened
1/4 cup sugar
1 teaspoon vanilla extract
10 to 12 slices white bread, crusts trimmed
1 dash of nutmeg or cinnamon

Slice the peaches into halves. Cut each half horizontally into 1/4-inch-thick slices. Combine the eggs, half-and-half, 1/2 cup sugar and 1 teaspoon vanilla in a mixing bowl. Beat until smooth. Combine the cream cheese, 1/4 cup sugar and 1 teaspoon vanilla in a mixing bowl. Beat until smooth.

Layer half the bread, half the egg mixture, the cream cheese mixture and peaches in a greased 11×17-inch baking dish. Continue layering with the remaining bread and the remaining egg mixture. Sprinkle with the nutmeg. Chill, covered with foil, for 8 to 10 hours. Let stand at room temperature for 30 minutes. Bake, covered, at 350 degrees for 30 to 40 minutes or until puffy and golden brown. Serve with warm maple syrup, if desired.

Serves 6

Breakfast Blintzes

This recipe was submitted by the Junior Auxiliary of Columbia, Tennessee. The JA of Columbia's project, MY CASA, works through the local courts to assist abused and neglected children.

1 cup sugar
4 teaspoons cinnamon
8 ounces cream cheese, softened
1/2 cup sugar

2 egg yolks
2 large loaves white bread, sliced
   and crusts trimmed
1 cup (2 sticks) margarine, melted

Mix 1 cup sugar and the cinnamon in a shallow dish. Combine the cream cheese, 1/2 cup sugar and the egg yolks in a mixing bowl. Beat until creamy, scraping the side of the bowl as needed. Flatten each slice of bread with a rolling pin. Spread one side of each slice of bread thinly with the cream cheese mixture. Roll each lengthwise to enclose the filling. Dip in the margarine and roll in the cinnamon-sugar. Arrange on a baking sheet and freeze until firm. Place in resealable plastic freezer bags. Freeze until baking time. Do not thaw before baking. Bake at 400 degrees for 15 minutes.

SERVES 15

Peanut Butter French Toast

1 loaf French bread, cut into
   16 slices
1/2 cup chunky peanut butter
4 eggs, beaten
1/4 cup heavy cream
2 teaspoons vanilla extract

4 cups sweetened cornflakes,
   finely crushed
1/4 cup (1/2 stick) butter, or
   as needed
Confectioners' sugar

Spread one side of eight slices of bread with the peanut butter. Top each with a slice of bread. Mix the eggs, cream and vanilla in a shallow dish. Place the cornflakes in a shallow dish. Lightly soak each sandwich in the egg mixture, turning once to coat. Dredge in the cornflakes and press them into the sandwiches. Cook the sandwiches in batches in butter in a skillet for 4 to 6 minutes or until brown on both sides, turning once. Add additional butter as needed. Place on a foil- or waxed paper-lined baking sheet and keep warm in a low-temperature oven until all the sandwiches have been cooked. Dust with confectioners' sugar. Serve with maple syrup.

SERVES 6 TO 8

"...we accept our membership as a commitment—A COMMITMENT VOLUNTARILY MADE BUT UNWAVERINGLY PURSUED."

—HELEN RIDLEY,
NAJA CROWNLET,
1968–1969

Baked French Toast with Streusel Topping

*This recipe is from the Junior Auxiliary of Philadelphia, Mississippi.
The JA of Philadelphia maintains a local playground with the* IMAGINATION
FUN STATION PLAYGROUND *program.*

    1 loaf bread, sliced
    10 to 12 eggs
    2 cups milk
    2 cups half-and-half
    1 tablespoon vanilla extract
    2 tablespoons cinnamon
    1 tablespoon nutmeg
    1/2 cup (1 stick) margarine, softened
    1 cup packed brown sugar
    2 to 4 tablespoons light corn syrup
    1/2 cup chopped pecans

Layer the bread three slices thick in a 9×13-inch baking dish. Mix the eggs, milk, half-and-half, vanilla, cinnamon and nutmeg in a bowl. Pour over the bread. Chill, covered, for 8 to 10 hours. Mix the margarine, brown sugar, corn syrup and pecans in a bowl. Spread over the French toast. Bake, covered with foil, at 350 degrees for 1 hour. Let stand for 15 minutes before slicing.

SERVES 10 TO 12

Eggs Benedict Casserole

"Through my service in
Junior Auxiliary, a
remarkable thing has
happened in my life.
I have been blessed and
humbled by the children
we've served, and by the
women with whom I serve
in carrying out our projects.
I see my own children in
these dear ones and I want
them to receive all the love
and hope that they truly
deserve. We are serving
God by serving the children
of our communities."

—ACTIVE MEMBER,
JA OF OXFORD

The Junior Auxiliary of Oxford, Mississippi, submitted this recipe. The JA of Oxford won the Louise Eskrigge Crump Award in 2007 for the ADOPT-A-FAMILY *project to supply one-on-one assistance to needy families.*

CASSEROLE
20 to 24 ounces Canadian bacon
6 English muffins
3 eggs
2 cups milk
1 teaspoon onion powder
$1/2$ teaspoon paprika

EASY HOLLANDAISE SAUCE
4 egg yolks
$1/2$ cup (1 stick) butter
$1/2$ cup whipping cream
2 to 3 teaspoons lemon juice

To prepare the casserole, chop the Canadian bacon into $1/2$-inch pieces. Cut the English muffins into $1/2$-inch pieces. Mix the eggs, milk and onion powder in a bowl. Layer half the Canadian bacon, the English muffins, remaining Canadian bacon and the egg mixture in a lightly greased 9×13-inch baking dish. Chill, covered, for 8 to 10 hours. Sprinkle with the paprika. Bake, covered with foil, at 375 degrees for 40 minutes or until the center is set.

To prepare the sauce, combine the egg yolks and one-third of the butter in the top of a double boiler. Place over boiling water. Cook until the butter melts, stirring constantly. Melt the remaining butter in a small saucepan over low heat. Add to the egg yolk mixture gradually, stirring constantly until blended. Remove from the heat and stir in the whipping cream and lemon juice. Serve warm over the casserole.

SERVES 10 TO 12

Governors' Eggs

The Junior Auxiliary of Clarksville, Tennessee, submitted this recipe from the chapter's cookbook, Linen Napkins to Paper Plates. *The JA of Clarksville provides layette baskets for newborns of needy families through the* Healthy Start *project.*

3 (10-ounce) packages frozen
    chopped spinach
8 slices bacon
1 cup chopped ham
1/4 cup (1/2 stick) butter
1 cup all-purpose flour
4 cups milk
2 teaspoons minced onion

Salt and pepper to taste
18 eggs
1 1/2 cups evaporated milk
1/4 cup (1/2 stick) butter
1/2 cup French-fried onion
    rings, crushed
1/2 cup (2 ounces) shredded
    Monterey Jack cheese

Prepare the spinach according to the package directions. Drain very well and finely chop. Cut the bacon into 1/4-inch pieces. Cook in a skillet until very crisp; drain, reserving the drippings. Cook the ham in the reserved drippings for 2 minutes, stirring occasionally; drain, reserving the drippings. Add 1/4 cup butter to the drippings and stir until melted. Add the flour gradually, stirring constantly until combined. Bring to a boil, stirring constantly. Add the milk gradually, stirring constantly until smooth. Cook until thickened, stirring constantly. Stir in the spinach and onion. Season with salt and pepper. Remove from the heat.

Combine the eggs and evaporated milk in a bowl. Season with salt and pepper. Whisk until frothy. Melt 1/4 cup butter in a skillet. Add the egg mixture and scramble until lightly set. Layer the eggs, bacon, ham and spinach mixture one-half at a time in a buttered 9×13-inch baking dish. Top with the onion rings and cheese. Chill, covered, for 8 to 10 hours. Bake at 275 degrees for 1 hour.

Serves 8 to 10

Southwestern Egg Casserole

"Junior Auxiliary takes ordinary, concerned citizens and provides resources to accomplish extraordinary things that touch the lives of children."

—Mary Carole Bowers

1 onion, chopped
1/4 cup (or more) olive oil
1 (16-ounce) package frozen shredded potatoes, thawed
16 eggs, beaten
1 cup milk
1 (10-ounce) can cream of mushroom soup
1 (4-ounce) can chopped green chiles, drained
1 teaspoon herb and spice seasoning blend
Salt and pepper to taste
1 cup (4 ounces) shredded Colby cheese
1 cup (4 ounces) shredded Monterey Jack cheese

Sauté the onion in the olive oil in a large skillet until tender and brown. Add the potatoes and cook until light brown, stirring frequently. Add additional olive oil as needed to prevent the potatoes from sticking to the skillet.

Whisk the eggs and milk in a bowl until frothy. Scramble in a large nonstick skillet until lightly set. Stir in the soup, green chiles and seasoning blend. Season with salt and pepper. Cook until the eggs are cooked through, stirring constantly; do not overcook.

Layer the potato mixture, half the Colby cheese, half the Monterey Jack cheese and the egg mixture in an 11×13-inch baking dish sprayed with nonstick cooking spray. Top with the remaining Colby cheese and the rermaining Monterey Jack cheese. Bake at 350 degrees for 25 minutes.

Serves 12 to 15

Hash Brown Breakfast Casserole

1 pound bulk pork sausage
5 eggs, beaten
1 cup Velveeta cheese, chopped
1 (10-ounce) can cream of
   celery soup

1 1/2 cups hash brown potatoes
2 tablespoons chopped onion
2 tablespoons chopped bell pepper
Salt and pepper to taste

Brown the sausage in a skillet, stirring until crumbly; drain. Let stand until cool. Mix the eggs, cheese, soup, potatoes, onion and bell pepper in a bowl. Stir in the sausage. Season with salt and pepper. Spoon into a greased 9×13-inch baking dish. Bake at 350 degrees for 45 minutes or until the center is set. The casserole may be prepared ahead and chilled, covered, until baking time. Bake for 1 hour if the casserole has been chilled.

Serves 8 to 10

Christmas Morning Egg Casserole

The Junior Auxiliary of Forrest City, Arkansas, contributed the following recipe. The JA of Forrest City selects one classroom each year for the JA Gems project to teach enrichment lessons in hygiene, etiquette, respect, and compassion.

7 slices white bread, crusts
   trimmed and bread chopped
2 cups (8 ounces) shredded
   Cheddar cheese
6 eggs
2 to 3 cups milk

1 teaspoon dry mustard
1/2 teaspoon salt
1/4 teaspoon pepper
1 pound bacon, crisp-cooked
   and crumbled

Combine the bread and cheese in a greased 7×11-inch baking dish. Whisk the eggs, milk, dry mustard, salt and pepper in a bowl until frothy. Pour over the bread and cheese. Sprinkle with the bacon. Chill, covered, for 8 to 10 hours. Let stand for 30 minutes before baking. Bake at 350 degrees for 50 to 55 minutes or until a knife inserted in the center comes out clean.

Serves 6 to 8

Cheesy Asparagus Tart

*"My fondest memory of JA
is the Christmas parade.
Wanting to be a good
member, I agreed to be
Frosty the Snowman, not
realizing how awkward
the costume would be.
My friend, Bugs Bunny,
also could not see in her
costume when she ran into
the policeman. 'Whoa,
Bugs, go that-a-way!'
Fortunately, our faces were
hidden and no one knew the
identity of the wayward
Bugs and Frosty."*

—Johnna Walker

1 1/2 pounds asparagus
1 (2-crust) refrigerator pie pastry
1 large sweet onion, chopped
1 tablespoon butter
2 tablespoons Dijon mustard
2 cups (8 ounces) shredded Colby-Monterey
   Jack cheese blend
1 1/2 cups half-and-half
2 eggs
1/4 teaspoon salt
1/4 teaspoon freshly ground pepper

Snap off the woody ends of the asparagus spears. Cook in boiling water in a saucepan for 30 seconds; drain. Plunge the asparagus into ice water to stop the cooking process; drain. Reserve nine attractive spears. Chop the remaining spears.

Unfold the pie pastries. Stack on a lightly floured surface. Roll into a 14-inch circle. Fit into an 11-inch tart pan and trim the edge. Line the tart shell with foil. Place pie weights or dried beans in the tart shell. Place on a baking sheet. Bake at 425 degrees for 12 minutes. Remove the foil and weights. Bake for 2 minutes longer. Cool on a wire rack.

Sauté the onion in the butter in a skillet over medium-high heat for 5 minutes or until tender. Brush the bottom and side of the tart shell with the Dijon mustard. Layer half the cheese, the chopped asparagus, onion and remaining cheese in the tart shell. Arrange the reserved asparagus spears on top. Whisk the half-and-half, eggs, salt and pepper in a bowl until frothy. Pour over the asparagus. Bake at 375 degrees for 25 minutes or until the center is set and the top is golden brown. Let stand for 15 minutes.

Serves 6 to 8

Quiche Lorraine

The Junior Auxiliary of Benton, Arkansas, contributed this recipe from the chapter's cookbook, CALICO CUPBOARDS. *The JA of Benton received the NAJA Presidents Award for 2003–04.*

6 thin slices onion
1 unbaked (9-inch) pie shell
4 eggs
1/4 teaspoon dry mustard
1 1/3 cups light cream, heated
6 slices bacon, crisp-cooked and chopped
8 paper-thin slices ham, shredded
8 paper-thin slices Swiss cheese
2 tablespoons browned butter
1/4 cup (1 ounce) grated Parmesan cheese

Sauté the onion in a skillet until soft. Do not prick the pie shell. Line the pie shell with foil. Place pie weights or dried beads in the pastry shell. Bake at 450 degrees for 8 minutes. Remove the foil and weights.

Mix the eggs and dry mustard in a bowl. Add the hot cream gradually, stirring constantly until blended. Layer the bacon, onion, half the ham and half the Swiss cheese in the pie shell. Continue layering with the remaining ham, the remaining Swiss cheese and the egg mixture. Let stand for 10 minutes. Bake at 350 degrees for 25 minutes. Drizzle with the browned butter and top with the Parmesan cheese. Bake for 10 minutes longer. Let stand for 10 minutes before slicing.

SERVES 6 TO 8

Tomato and Wild Rice Quiche

The very heart of Junior
Auxiliary lies within the
projects of each chapter . . .
Although the classifications
are uniform . . . social,
welfare, educational, cultural,
and civic . . . there are
dozens of different types of
work being carried on
throughout our National
Association.

—NAJA Crownlet, 1965

2 (6-ounce) packages long grain wild rice
2 eggs
1 tablespoon water
4 unbaked (9-inch) pie shells
3 garlic cloves, minced
2 tablespoons olive oil
1 (14-ounce) can chopped Italian-style tomatoes
16 ounces cream cheese, softened and cut into pieces
1^1/$_2$ teaspoons salt
1^1/$_2$ teaspoons pepper
8 eggs, beaten

Cook the rice according to the package directions. Whisk 2 eggs and the water lightly in a bowl until combined. Brush the bottoms, sides and crusts of the pie shells with the egg wash. Bake at 400 degrees for 3 minutes.

Sauté the garlic in the olive oil in a skillet until light brown. Add the rice, tomatoes and cream cheese. Cook until the cream cheese is melted, stirring constantly. Season with the salt and pepper. Remove from the heat. Add eight eggs gradually, stirring constantly. Pour into the pie shells. Bake at 375 degrees for 25 minutes. This dish freezes well.

Serves 20

Sausage Bread

2 loaves frozen bread
1 pound hot bulk pork sausage
1 pound mild bulk pork sausage
8 ounces mozzarella
   cheese, shredded
8 ounces Cheddar cheese, shredded

1 dash of oregano
1 dash of basil
1 dash of salt
1 dash of pepper
1 egg, beaten

Thaw the bread and let rise according to the package directions. Cook the sausage in a skillet until crumbly; drain. Mix the sausage, mozzarella cheese, Cheddar cheese, oregano, basil, salt and pepper in bowl. Roll out each loaf of dough into a rectangle $1/2$ inch thick. Spread half the sausage mixture over each loaf. Roll the dough lengthwise to enclose the filling. Place seam side down on a baking sheet. Brush the tops with the egg. Bake at 350 degrees for 30 minutes or until golden brown.

SERVES 8

Cranberry Bread

2 cups all-purpose flour
$3/4$ cup sugar
$1 1/2$ teaspoons baking powder
1 teaspoon salt
$1/2$ teaspoon baking soda
1 egg, beaten

1 teaspoon grated orange zest
$3/4$ cup orange juice
2 tablespoons vegetable oil
1 cup frozen cranberries, thawed
   and chopped
$1/2$ cup pecans, chopped

Sift the flour, sugar, baking powder, salt and baking soda together. Mix the egg, orange zest, orange juice and oil in a large bowl. Stir in the flour mixture. Fold in the cranberries and pecans. Spoon into a greased 5×9-inch loaf pan. Bake at 350 degrees for 45 minutes or until golden brown. Cool in the pan for 15 minutes.

SERVES 12

Zucchini Bread

This recipe is a favorite if the Junior Auxiliary of Ruston, Louisiana. The JA of Ruston makes Huggy Bears *for children who are patients in local hospitals.*

1 cup vegetable oil	1 teaspoon baking soda
3 eggs, lightly beaten	1/4 teaspoon baking powder
2 cups sugar	1 teaspoon salt
1 cup grated zucchini	1 tablespoon cinnamon
2 teaspoons vanilla extract	1 cup chopped pecans or walnuts
2 cups all-purpose flour	

Mix the oil, eggs, sugar, zucchini and vanilla in a large bowl by hand. Stir in the flour, baking soda, baking powder, salt, cinnamon and pecans. Pour into two greased loaf pans. Bake at 325 degrees for 1 1/2 hours. This bread is very moist and not too sweet, and it freezes well.

Serves 24

Nutty Orange Coffee Cake

3/4 cup granulated sugar	2 (10-count) cans
1/2 cup chopped pecans	buttermilk biscuits
2 teaspoons grated orange zest	1/2 cup (1 stick) butter, melted
4 ounces cream cheese	1 cup confectioners' sugar
	2 tablespoons orange juice

Mix the granulated sugar, pecans and orange zest in a bowl. Spoon approximately 3/4 teaspoon cream cheese onto the center of each biscuit and fold in half, pinching the edges together to seal. Dip in the butter and dredge in the pecan mixture. Arrange tightly in a single layer curved side down in a bundt pan. Place any remaining biscuits around the center of the pan. Drizzle with the remaining butter and sprinkle with the remaining pecan mixture. Bake at 350 degrees for 35 minutes. Invert onto a serving plate immediately. Mix the confectioners' sugar and orange juice in a bowl. Drizzle over the warm coffee cake.

Serves 12

Lemon Cream Cheese Coffee Cake

1 envelope dry yeast
1/4 cup warm water
2 cups all-purpose flour
1/8 teaspoon salt
3/4 cup margarine
1 egg, lightly beaten
16 ounces cream cheese, softened
1 1/2 cups granulated sugar
2 tablespoons grated lemon zest, or
   1 1/2 teaspoons lemon juice
Confectioners' sugar

Dissolve the yeast in the water in a bowl. Mix the flour and salt in a bowl. Cut in the margarine with a pastry blender until crumbly. Add the yeast mixture and egg; mix well. Divide the pastry into two equal portions. Roll each portion into a 14×20-inch rectangle. Beat the cream cheese, granulated sugar and lemon zest in a bowl until light and creamy. Spread over each pastry to within 1 to 2 inches of the edge. Roll each as for a jelly roll from the short side. Pinch the edges together and place seam side down on a baking sheet. Cut a slit in the tops to allow steam to escape. Bake at 375 degrees for 25 to 30 minutes or until light brown. Dust with confectioners' sugar.

SERVES 12

49

"Our first duty is still to the children of our own community. It is our duty to clothe them, feed them, and give them medical care. If we are to build a better America tomorrow, it must be with the children on our doorsteps today . . . think of your purpose as two-fold, the saving of America for the children you are caring for today, that they may build the America of tomorrow."

—LOUISE ESKRIGGE CRUMP

Cinnamon Scones

1 cup sour cream	2 teaspoons baking powder
1 teaspoon baking soda	1/2 teaspoon cream of tartar
1 egg, lightly beaten	1 teaspoon salt
4 teaspoons cinnamon	1 cup (2 sticks) butter, chopped
4 cups all-purpose flour	Cinnamon
1 cup sugar	Sugar

Mix the sour cream and baking soda in a small bowl. Stir in the egg and 4 teaspoons cinnamon. Mix the flour, 1 cup sugar, the baking powder, cream of tartar and salt in a bowl. Cut in the butter until crumbly. Stir in the sour cream mixture gently. Knead the dough eight to ten times or until it holds together. Divide the dough into two equal portions and place each on a baking sheet sprayed with nonstick cooking spray. Pat each into a 3/4-inch-thick circle. Slice each into six wedges or cut with a biscuit cutter. Rearrange so that they do not touch. Mix equal amounts of cinnamon and sugar in a bowl. Sprinkle over the dough. Bake at 350 degrees for 15 to 20 minutes or until golden brown.

SERVES 12 TO 16

Breakfast Rolls

1/2 cup pecans, chopped	1/2 cup (1 stick) butter, melted
24 freezer dinner rolls	1/2 cup packed brown sugar
1 (4-ounce) package butterscotch cook-and-serve pudding mix	1 tablespoon cinnamon

Layer the pecans, rolls and pudding mix in a greased bundt pan. Mix the butter, brown sugar and cinnamon in a bowl. Pour over the pudding mix. Cover with plastic wrap sprayed with nonstick cooking spray. Let stand for 8 to 10 hours. Remove the plastic wrap. Bake at 350 degrees for 30 minutes. Invert onto a lipped serving plate.

MAKES 24

Cheddar Cheese and Sausage Muffins

This recipe is from the Junior Auxiliary of Monticello, Arkansas. The JA of Monticello instructs children at the local children's home during the chapter's CHRISTMAS CRAFTS *project.*

8 ounces bulk pork sausage
1 1/2 cups baking mix
1/2 teaspoon cayenne pepper

1/2 cup milk
1/2 cup (2 ounces) shredded
   Cheddar cheese

Brown the sausage in a skillet, stirring until crumbly; drain. Mix the baking mix and cayenne pepper in a bowl. Stir in the milk. Add the sausage and cheese; mix well. The mixture will be very thick. Spoon into greased miniature muffin cups. Bake at 400 degrees for 12 minutes.

MAKES 24

Banana Crunch Muffins

3 cups all-purpose flour
2 cups sugar
2 teaspoons baking powder
1 teaspoon baking soda
1/2 teaspoon salt
1 cup (2 sticks) butter, melted
2 extra-large eggs
3/4 cup milk

2 teaspoons vanilla extract
1 cup mashed bananas
   (about 2 bananas)
1 cup chopped banana
1 cup chopped walnuts
1 cup granola without raisins
1 cup shredded sweetened coconut
Dried banana chips (optional)

Lightly grease the top of a large muffin pan and line the cups with paper liners. Sift the flour, sugar, baking powder, baking soda and salt into a mixing bowl. Add the butter and beat with a paddle attachment until combined. Mix the eggs, milk, vanilla and mashed bananas in a bowl. Add to the flour mixture and beat until combined. Do not overmix. Fold in the chopped banana, walnuts, granola and coconut. Spoon into the prepared pan. Top each muffin with dried banana chips, additional granola or additional coconut. Bake at 350 degrees for 25 to 30 minutes or until the tops are brown and a wooden pick inserted in the centers comes out clean. Cool slightly in the pan.

MAKES 18

"Joe lived at a shelter for abused children who have been removed from their homes. The children who earned points for good behavior participated in our Saturday visits. Joe was always present, telling us it was his last visit because he was going home. Finally his wish came true; his grandmother was taking Joe home. We filled a suitcase for him and hugged him good-bye—one more life improved!"

—CAROL CARUSO

South Mississippi Spice Muffins

The Junior Auxiliary of Gulfport, Mississippi, donated this recipe. The JA of Gulfport won the 2007 Martha Wise Award for MIRACLE IN THE PARK, *a project to rebuild a local playground after Hurricane Katrina.*

4 cups all-purpose flour
2 teaspoons baking soda
1 cup (2 sticks) butter, softened
2 cups sugar
2 eggs
2 cups applesauce

1 tablespoon cinnamon
2 teaspoons ground allspice
1 teaspoon ground cloves
1 teaspoon salt
1 cup chopped pecans

Sift the flour and baking soda together. Cream the butter and sugar in a mixing bowl until light and fluffy. Add the eggs and beat until smooth. Add the applesauce, cinnamon, allspice, cloves and salt. Beat until combined. Add the flour mixture and beat until combined. Stir in the pecans. Spoon into greased miniature muffin cups. Bake at 350 degrees for 8 to 10 minutes. The batter freezes well.

MAKES 3 DOZEN

Sweet Potato Muffins

1/2 cup margarine, softened
3/4 cup packed brown sugar
1 cup cooked puréed sweet potato
1 egg
1/4 cup molasses

11/2 cups all-purpose flour
1 teaspoon baking soda
1/4 teaspoon salt
1/2 cup chopped pecans (optional)

Cream the margarine and brown sugar in a mixing bowl until light and fluffy. Add the sweet potato, egg and molasses. Beat until combined. Combine the flour, baking soda and salt. Add to the sweet potato mixture and beat until combined. Stir in the pecans. Spoon into greased muffin cups, filling each cup three-fourths full. Bake at 400 degrees for 18 minutes. For a variation, cooked puréed pumpkin may be substituted for the sweet potato.

SERVES 16

Buttery Herb Cheese Muffins

2 cups self-rising flour
1 cup (2 sticks) butter, melted
1 (6-ounce) package garlic and herb
   spreadable cheese, softened
1/2 cup sour cream

Mix the flour, butter, cheese and sour cream in a bowl until smooth. Spoon into lightly greased miniature muffin cups, filling to the top. Bake at 350 degrees for 25 minutes or until light brown.

MAKES 2¹/2 DOZEN

Broccoli Corn Bread Muffins

2 (8-ounce) packages corn bread mix
1 (10-ounce) package frozen chopped
   broccoli, thawed
4 eggs, lightly beaten
1 cup cottage cheese
1 onion, chopped
1 cup (2 sticks) margarine, melted
1/2 cup (2 ounces) shredded Cheddar cheese

Mix the corn bread mix, broccoli, eggs, cottage cheese, onion and margarine in a bowl. Spoon into greased muffin cups. Sprinkle with the cheese. Bake at 375 degrees for 30 to 35 minutes or until light brown.

MAKES 12 TO 16

Creole Corn Bread

"Why do we call ourselves
Junior Auxiliary? Although
no one really knows for sure,
the dictionary definitions of
the two separate words make
perfect sense in combination.
The definition of the word
Junior *most fitting to
our group is 'intended
for or including young
people or children.' And,
the word* Auxiliary *means
'providing assistance;
helping.' That is a perfect
fit for JA and what we do!"*

—ACTIVE MEMBER,
JA OF BROOKHAVEN

1 (1-pound) package frozen crawfish tails, thawed,
   or 1 pound peeled shrimp
Olive oil
Creole seasoning blend to taste
1/2 cup sour cream
1/2 cup milk
1 egg, beaten
1/4 cup (1/2 stick) butter, melted
1 cup cornmeal
1 cup all-purpose flour
1 tablespoon baking powder
1 teaspoon salt
1/2 teaspoon baking soda
1/2 cup chopped red bell pepper
1 bunch green onions, chopped
1 tablespoon seeded chopped jalapeño chile
1/2 cup (2 ounces) shredded Monterey Jack cheese

Sauté the crawfish in olive oil in a skillet until the crawfish turn pink. Season with the Creole seasoning while cooking. Whisk the sour cream, milk, egg and butter in a bowl until smooth. Add the cornmeal, flour, baking powder, salt and baking soda. Stir until all lumps are gone. Stir in the crawfish, bell pepper, green onions and jalapeño chile. Pour into a greased 10-inch skillet. Sprinkle with the cheese. Bake at 400 degrees for 30 minutes or until golden brown.

SERVES 6 TO 8

French Onion Biscuits

1 (8-ounce) container French
    onion dip
1/4 cup milk

1 tablespoon finely chopped parsley
2 cups all-purpose baking mix
1 tablespoon butter, melted

Whisk the French onion dip, milk and parsley in a bowl until combined. Add the baking mix and mix well. Spoon into twelve equal portions on a lightly greased baking sheet. Brush the tops with the butter. Bake at 450 degrees for 7 to 8 minutes or until light golden brown. Let stand on the baking sheet for 5 minutes.

MAKES 12

Little Teeny Do-Ahead Biscuits

1 cup (2 sticks) butter, melted
1 cup sour cream

2 cups self-rising flour

Mix the butter, sour cream and flour in a bowl. Drop by spoonfuls into miniature muffin cups. Bake for 350 degrees for 25 minutes. These freeze well after baking.

MAKES ABOUT 2 DOZEN

Rise-and-Shine Biscuits

1 tablespoon plus
  2 teaspoons sugar
1/3 cup sour cream

1/3 cup club soda
2 cups baking mix

Mix the sugar, sour cream and club soda in a bowl. Stir in the baking mix. Knead ten to twelve times on a lightly floured surface. Shape the dough into six biscuits and place in a lightly greased round cake pan. Bake at 450 degrees for 16 to 18 minutes.

MAKES 6

Tomato Basil Biscuits

The Junior Auxiliary of Louisville, Mississippi, submitted this recipe from TASTING TEA. *The JA of Louisville supplies clothes for any child who might need a change of clothes while at school in the* WEE CARE *project.*

1 cup all-purpose flour
2 tablespoons baking powder
1/2 teaspoon salt
1/4 teaspoon sugar
1/4 cup (1/2 stick) unsalted butter

2 tomatoes, peeled, seeded
  and chopped
1/4 cup half-and-half
1/3 cup chopped fresh basil

Mix the flour, baking powder, salt and sugar in a bowl. Cut in the butter until crumbly. Stir in the tomatoes, half-and-half and basil. Knead the dough on a floured surface for 30 seconds. Roll 1 inch thick and cut into desired shape. Bake at 425 degrees for 15 minutes or until golden brown.

MAKES 1 DOZEN

JA of Paragould undertakes a project, CHRISTMAS BLESSING, *which provides Christmas gifts for needy children. Schools supply a list of the children's needs. During a party for the children, complete with Santa, entertainment, and goodies, the parents privately receive gifts they can share with their children on Christmas morning. Grown men's tears and touching notes of thanks all fuel the fire for our volunteers to work hard to impact those important lives.*

Yeast Biscuits

1 envelope dry yeast
1 cup warm water
1 egg, beaten
1 teaspoon salt

3 tablespoons sugar
2 1/2 to 2 3/4 cups all-purpose flour
2 tablespoons margarine, melted
Melted butter

Dissolve the yeast in the water in a bowl. Beat the egg, salt and sugar in a mixing bowl until smooth. Add the yeast mixture and beat until combined. Add half the flour gradually, beating constantly at low speed until combined. Add the margarine and beat until combined. Add the remaining flour gradually, beating constantly at low speed until combined. Knead on a floured surface until easy to handle. Roll out. Cut with a biscuit cutter and dip in melted butter. Fold each biscuit in half and arrange in a baking pan. Let rise for 1 hour. Bake at 425 degrees for 12 to 15 minutes.

Makes 2 1/2 dozen

Yeast Hot Rolls

1/2 cup boiling water
1/2 cup (1 stick) butter
1/3 cup sugar
1 teaspoon salt
1 1/4 tablespoons dry yeast
1/2 cup lukewarm water

1 egg
3 cups all-purpose flour
Melted butter
Garlic powder or sesame seeds
(optional)

Combine 1/2 cup boiling water, 1/2 cup butter, the sugar and salt in a large bowl and stir until the butter is melted and the sugar and salt are dissolved. Let stand until cool. Dissolve the yeast in 1/2 cup lukewarm water in a bowl and beat in the egg. Add to the butter mixture. Add the flour and mix well. Chill, covered, for 8 to 10 hours. Roll out on a lightly floured surface and cut into rolls. Use as little flour as possible. Place on a baking sheet. Let stand for 2 hours. Brush the tops with melted butter and sprinkle with garlic powder. Bake at 425 degrees for 12 minutes or until golden brown.

Makes 3 dozen

Rosemary Focaccia

*"The most elegant dish I
ever saw on a table was at
the cocktail party for early
arrivals before a regional JA
meeting many years ago. A
silver tray, lined with fresh
lettuce, mounded with
steamed asparagus and
whole artichokes, tiny red
tomatoes, and centered with
a bowl of Hollandaise, it
was simple yet opulent. The
image remained long after
the party was over."*

—LYN PATRICK

1 envelope dry yeast
1¹/2 cups warm water (105 to 115 degrees)
5 cups all-purpose flour
¹/4 cup olive oil
2¹/2 teaspoons salt
1 to 2 tablespoons all-purpose flour
3 tablespoons olive oil
1 tablespoon finely chopped fresh rosemary
1 teaspoon coarse sea salt

Dissolve the yeast in the water in the mixing bowl of a stand mixer. Let stand
for 5 minutes. Add 5 cups flour, ¹/4 cup olive oil and 2¹/2 teaspoons salt. Beat at
medium speed with a whisk attachment until combined. Beat at medium speed
with a hook attachment or knead by hand for 3 to 4 minutes or until a smooth
sticky dough forms. Turn out onto a lightly floured surface. Knead in 1 to
2 tablespoons flour. Place in a bowl coated with additional olive oil, turning to
coat. Cover with plastic wrap. Let rise in a warm place for 1¹/2 hours or until
doubled in bulk.

Press the dough into a 10×15-inch baking pan coated with additional olive oil.
Cover with a kitchen towel and let rise for 1 hour or until doubled in bulk.
Make indentations in the top of the dough with fingertips. Mix 3 tablespoons olive
oil and the rosemary in a bowl. Brush generously over the dough, letting the oil
pool in the indentations. Sprinkle with 1 teaspoon sea salt. Bake at 450 degrees
for 20 to 25 minutes or until golden brown. Invert onto a wire rack. Serve warm
or at room temperature.

SERVES 8 TO 10

Dilly Casserole Bread

1 envelope dry yeast
1/4 cup warm water
1 cup creamed cottage cheese
1 egg, lightly beaten
2 tablespoons sugar
1 tablespoon butter, melted
1 tablespoon onion flakes
2 teaspoons dill seeds
1 teaspoon salt
1/4 teaspoon baking soda
2 1/4 cups all-purpose flour
Melted butter
Salt to taste

Sprinkle the yeast over the water in a bowl. Let stand for 5 minutes. Stir until dissolved. Heat the cottage cheese until lukewarm. Mix the yeast mixture, cottage cheese, egg, sugar, butter, onion flakes, dill seeds, 1 teaspoon salt and the baking soda in a bowl. Add the flour and stir until a soft dough forms. Cover and let rise for 1 hour or until doubled in bulk. Punch the dough down and place in a greased 1 1/2-quart baking dish. Let rise for 40 minutes or until light. Bake at 350 degrees for 40 minutes or until golden brown. Brush with melted butter and sprinkle with salt to taste.

Serves 6 to 8

Salads &
Soups

NAJA National Scholarship Program

The NAJA National Scholarship Program was established in 1962, and the first grant of $2,000 was awarded in August of that year. But it was Betty Robbins, NAJA President 1992–93, who saw the value of growing the NAJA Scholarship Program, not only through increased giving, but by telling its story.

She chose to make the Scholarship Program her theme for the year she was president. She hoped that when she finished her term as ex officio, she could continue to serve the Association on the Scholarship Committee, even though she knew she was ill at the time. The subsequent death of Betty Robbins in January 1995 inspired an outpouring of generosity from her family and friends to the Scholarship Fund that has been unsurpassed in this Association to this day. Her husband and sons, knowing of her love for JA, and particularly her desire to help others through the Scholarship Program, chose to honor her by making a substantial contribution in her memory in 1995. ➤

Since that time, her family has donated more than $100,000 to the program. Her husband sent a letter to friends and business associates informing them of Betty's commitment to the program and of the opportunity to contribute to a lasting memorial. In the year following her death, 241 donations were received, many of them quite substantial. In 1999 the Robbins family established the Betty Robbins Endowed Scholarship Fund as part of the NAJA National Scholarship Program and offered to match gifts to the fund up to $10,000 per year. Betty's legacy lives on through the program dedicated to her name that provides educators with the opportunity to significantly impact the lives of children.

Cinnamon Apple Salad

CINNAMON VINAIGRETTE

1/4 cup raspberry vinegar

1 teaspoon sugar

1 teaspoon Dijon mustard

1 teaspoon cinnamon

1/4 teaspoon salt

1/2 cup canola oil

SALAD

1 golden Delicious apple

2 teaspoons water

1 teaspoon cinnamon

1 (8- to 10-ounce) package mixed salad greens

2 ounces goat cheese, crumbled

3 tablespoons coarsely chopped walnuts

To prepare the vinaigrette, whisk the vinegar, sugar, Dijon mustard, cinnamon and salt in a bowl until blended. Add the canola oil in a fine stream, whisking constantly until mixed well.

To prepare the salad, core and slice the apple into quarters. Slice the quarters into 1/4-inch-thick slices. Mix the apple, water and cinnamon in a microwave-safe bowl. Microwave on High for 1 minute, stirring once. Let stand to cool for 10 minutes. Combine the salad greens and 1/2 cup of the vinaigrette in a bowl; toss until coated. Divide among four salad plates. Top with the apple mixture, goat cheese and walnuts. Serve the remaining salad dressing on the side or store in a sealed container in the refrigerator for up to 1 week.

SERVES 4

Autumn Apple Salad

1 (20-ounce) can crushed pineapple
2/3 cup sugar
1 (3-ounce) package lemon gelatin
8 ounces cream cheese, softened
1 cup chopped apple

1 cup chopped celery
1 cup whipped topping
1/2 to 1 cup chopped pecans
Lettuce leaves

Combine the undrained pineapple and sugar in a saucepan. Bring to a boil and boil for 3 minutes, stirring occasionally. Remove from the heat. Add the gelatin and stir until dissolved. Add the cream cheese and stir until blended. Let stand until cool. Fold in the apple, celery, whipped topping and pecans. Pour into a 9×9-inch dish. Chill until firm. Cut into squares and serve on lettuce leaves.

SERVES 16

Blueberry Salad

DESSERTS, *the cookbook of the Junior Auxiliary of Grenada, Mississippi, includes this recipe. The JA of Grenada presents scholarships based on need and merit to graduating seniors each year with the chapter's* McCOOL SCHOLARSHIP *project.*

SALAD
2 small packages black cherry or
   blackberry gelatin
3 cups boiling water
1 (8-ounce) can sweetened crushed
   pineapple, drained
1 (22-ounce) can blueberry
   pie filling

TOPPING
8 ounces cream cheese, softened
1 cup sour cream
1/2 cup sugar
1/2 cup chopped pecans, toasted

To prepare the salad, dissolve the gelatin in the boiling water in a 9×13-inch glass dish. Stir in the pineapple and pie filling. Chill, covered, until firm.

To prepare the topping, combine the cream cheese, sour cream and sugar in a blender. Process until smooth. Stir in the pecans and spread over the salad. Sprinkle with additional toasted chopped pecans, if desired.

SERVES 15

"Jackson County JA members are known by local Wal-Mart employees for our infamous shopping adventures. It's fun to run into community members who also know what we're up to when they see us. Local elementary schools depend on our BACKPACK project to provide school supplies for underprivileged students. We provide CHRISTMAS BLESSINGS and EASTER BASKETS for the kids we serve and adore. We love what we do—and will shop until we drop!"

—ACTIVE MEMBER,
JA OF JACKSON COUNTY

Cranberry Salad

The Junior Auxiliary of Crittenden County, Arkansas, donated this recipe. The JA of Crittenden makes gift bags for pediatric patients at the local hospital through the chapter's Get Well Soon *project.*

1 pound cranberries
2 cups sugar
2 pints heavy whipping cream
2 cups chopped celery

1 cup pecans, chopped
2 cups miniature
   marshmallows, chopped

Chop the cranberries coarsely in a food processor fitted with a steel blade. Mix the cranberries and sugar in a bowl. Chill, covered, for 8 to 10 hours; drain. Beat the whipping cream in a mixing bowl until firm peaks form. Fold into the cranberry mixture. Fold in the celery, pecans and marshmallows one at a time. Chill, covered, for 1 hour.

Serves 12

Grape Salad

The Crown Jewels of JA, *the cookbook of the Junior Auxiliary of Milan, Tennessee, contains this recipe. The JA of Milan's* Patterson Picnic *project provides for chapter members to host a day of socialization and recreation for mentally impaired adults.*

8 cups seedless red grapes
8 ounces cream cheese, softened
1/2 cup sugar
1 teaspoon vanilla extract

1 cup sour cream
2 cups pecans, chopped
1/2 cup packed brown sugar

Arrange the grapes in a 9×13-inch glass dish lined with two layers of paper towels. Chill, covered with plastic wrap, for 8 to 10 hours. Remove the grapes and paper towels. Mix the cream cheese, sugar and vanilla in a bowl. Stir in the sour cream and grapes. Spoon into the 9×13-inch dish. Mix the pecans and brown sugar in a bowl. Spread over the grape mixture.

Serves 8 to 12

"Not only have I been blessed through being a part of the service we provide to the children of our community, but I also feel blessed by the relationships I've developed in the process. The best friends I have I would have never met had I not met them through the service of Junior Auxiliary."

—ACTIVE MEMBER,
JA OF JONESBORO

Grapefruit Salad with Celery Seed Dressing

CELERY SEED DRESSING
1/3 cup sugar
1/4 cup vinegar
2 teaspoons celery seeds
1 teaspoon dry mustard
1 teaspoon fresh lemon juice
1/2 teaspoon salt
1 cup vegetable oil, chilled

SALAD
1 (24-ounce) jar grapefruit
  sections, drained
2 to 3 avocados, sliced into wedges
1 head romaine, torn
1 large red onion, thinly sliced

To prepare the dressing, combine the sugar, vinegar, celery seeds, dry mustard, lemon juice and salt in a jar with a tight-fitting lid and seal tightly. Shake to mix. Add the oil in thirds, shaking to mix after each additon. Chill until serving time.

To prepare the salad, divide the grapefruit and avocado wedges equally on beds of the lettuce. Top with the red onion. Drizzle with the vinaigrette.

SERVES 6 TO 8

Fruit Salad with Blackberry Basil Vinaigrette

BLACKBERRY BASIL VINAIGRETTE
1/2 (10-ounce) jar seedless
  blackberry preserves
1/4 cup red wine vinegar
6 fresh basil leaves
1 garlic clove, thinly sliced
1/2 teaspoon salt
1/2 teaspoon seasoned pepper blend
3/4 cup vegetable oil

SALAD
8 cups mixed greens
1 1/2 cups sliced mangoes
1 1/2 cups grapefruit sections
1 1/2 cups sliced strawberries
1 cup blackberries
1 large avocado, sliced

To prepare the vinaigrette, combine the preserves, vinegar, basil, garlic, salt and seasoned pepper blend in a food processor and pulse until blended. Add the oil gradually, processing constantly until blended.

To prepare the salad, divide the salad greens among eight salad plates. Top with the mangoes, grapefruit, strawberries, blackberries and avocado. Drizzle with the vinaigrette.

SERVES 8

Romaine Salad with Strawberries and Honey Dressing

Honey Dressing

2/3 cup sugar

1/3 cup honey

1/3 cup apple cider vinegar

1 teaspoon grated onion

1 teaspoon dry mustard

1 teaspoon paprika

1 teaspoon celery seeds

1/4 teaspoon salt

1 cup canola oil

Salad

4 cups torn romaine
   or spinach

1 cup sliced strawberries, or
   1 (10-ounce) can
   mandarin oranges

1 cup crumbled feta cheese or
   blue cheese

1/2 cup crushed toasted pecans
   or almonds

To prepare the dressing, combine the sugar, honey, vinegar, onion, dry mustard, paprika, celery seeds and salt in a jar with a tight-fitting lid and seal tightly. Shake to mix. Add the canola oil. Seal tightly and shake to mix. Store in the refrigerator for up to 2 weeks. Bring to room temperature before serving.

To prepare the salad, combine the lettuce, strawberries, cheese and pecans in a large salad bowl. Add the salad dressing to taste and toss until coated. Serve immediately.

SERVES 4

Strawberry Spinach Salad

The Junior Auxiliary of Obion County, Tennessee, chose this recipe as a favorite. The JA of Obion County holds BOO BASH, *a Halloween carnival for children emphasizing safety.*

1/2 cup vegetable oil

1/4 cup red wine vinegar

1/4 cup sugar

1/4 teaspoon garlic powder

1/4 teaspoon onion powder

1/4 teaspoon dry mustard

Salt and pepper to taste

9 cups baby spinach leaves

1 pint strawberries, sliced

1/2 cup slivered almonds

Process the oil, vinegar, sugar, garlic powder, onion powder and dry mustard in a food processor until blended. Season with salt and pepper. Combine the spinach, strawberries and almonds in a bowl. Add the dressing and toss until coated. Serve immediately.

SERVES 6 TO 8

Black Bean Salad

DRESSING
1 small garlic clove
3 tablespoons lime juice
1/4 teaspoon chili powder
1/4 cup extra-virgin olive oil
Salt and freshly ground pepper
   to taste

SALAD
1 cup corn kernels (about 2 ears) or
   frozen corn kernels, thawed
1 orange bell pepper or red bell
   pepper, chopped
1 green bell pepper, chopped
   (optional)

1/2 small red onion, finely chopped
1 (15-ounce) can black beans,
   drained and rinsed
1 cup cherry tomatoes, cut into
   halves, or chopped Roma
   tomatoes
1 avocado, chopped
1/4 cup chopped fresh cilantro leaves
   and stems, or 1/4 cup chopped
   fresh parsley
Salt and freshly ground pepper
   to taste
1 tablespoon olive oil (optional)

To prepare the dressing, whisk the garlic, lime juice, chili powder and olive oil in a bowl until blended. Season with salt and pepper.

To prepare the salad, combine the corn, bell peppers, onion, beans, tomatoes, avocado and cilantro in a bowl. Add the dressing and toss until coated. Season with salt and pepper.

SERVES 12

Broccoli Salad

Florets of 1 bunch broccoli
2 cups cauliflower florets
1/4 to 1/2 red onion, chopped
12 slices bacon, crisp-cooked
   and crumbled
1 cup golden raisins
1/2 cup chopped walnuts

1 cup mayonnaise
1/2 cup sugar
2 to 3 tablespoons vinegar or apple
   cider vinegar
2 hard-cooked eggs, chopped
1 cup (4 ounces) shredded
   Cheddar cheese

Combine the broccoli, cauliflower, onion, bacon, raisins and walnuts in a large salad bowl. Mix the mayonnaise, sugar and vinegar in a bowl. Add to the broccoli mixture and toss until coated. Top with the eggs and cheese. Serve immediately.

SERVES 6

Marinated Coleslaw

2 cups apple cider vinegar
1 1/2 cups sugar
1 cup water
1 cup vegetable oil
1 head cabbage, chopped
4 green bell peppers, chopped
3 large Vidalia onions, chopped
Salt and pepper to taste

Whisk the vinegar, sugar, water and oil in a bowl until blended. Add the cabbage, bell peppers and onions; toss until coated. Season with salt and pepper. Chill, covered, for 24 hours; drain. Store in the refrigerator for up to 1 week. Drain as needed.

Serves 8 to 12

Cucumber Salad

4 large cucumbers, peeled and sliced
1 onion, sliced
1 cup mayonnaise
1/4 cup apple cider vinegar
1/2 cup sugar
1 teaspoon salt
1/2 teaspoon pepper

Layer the cucumbers and onion in a serving bowl. Mix the mayonnaise, vinegar, sugar, salt and pepper in a bowl. Pour over the onion. Chill, covered, for 2 hours. This salad can be made ahead and stored in the refrigerator for 3 or 4 days.

Serves 6 to 8

Hot Bacon Potato Salad

All of us are giving a great deal of our time to JA work. Therefore, it's a safe assumption that we believe in what we are doing. Yet, it behooves us to ask ourselves if we believe strongly enough . . . Through our Junior Auxiliary projects, we are performing community services of which we can be proud. In any community . . . someone must assume this burden . . . And above all, let's remember that the act of serving others is a God-given privilege!

—NAJA Crownlet, 1964

The Junior Auxiliary of Batesville, Mississippi, includes this recipe in the chapter's cookbook, Crown The Cook. *The JA of Batesville won the Louise Eskrigge Crump Award in 2003 for the* JA Buddies *project, and again in 2005 for the* Heart to Heart *project.*

5 potatoes (about 1 1/2 pounds)
8 slices bacon, crisp-cooked and crumbled
3 green onions, finely chopped
2 ribs celery, finely chopped (about 1 cup)
1/2 cup mayonnaise
1/4 cup vinegar
2 teaspoons sugar
1 teaspoon dry mustard
1 teaspoon salt
1/4 teaspoon coarsely ground pepper

Bring 1 inch of water to a boil in a 3-quart saucepan. Add the potatoes. Cover and return to a boil. Reduce the heat to low. Simmer for 25 minutes or until tender; drain. Slice the potatoes 1/4 inch thick. Mix the potatoes, bacon, green onions and celery in a large bowl. Mix the mayonnaise, vinegar, sugar, dry mustard, salt and pepper in a bowl. Pour over the potato mixture and toss until coated. Pour into an 8×8-inch baking pan lined with foil. Cover with foil and place on a grill rack 4 inches above medium-hot coals. Grill for 20 minutes, stirring once.

Serves 4 to 6

Lemon Pasta Salad

2/3 cup (3 ounces) freshly grated
  Parmesan cheese
1/2 cup lemon juice
1/2 cup olive oil
3/4 teaspoon salt
3/4 teaspoon pepper

1 pound angel hair pasta
Salt to taste
1 (2-ounce) can sliced black
  olives, drained
1/3 cup chopped fresh basil
1 tablespoon grated lemon zest

Whisk the cheese, lemon juice, olive oil, salt and pepper in a bowl. Cook the pasta in salted water in a large saucepan until tender. Drain, reserving 1 cup of the cooking liquid. Add the pasta to the cheese mixture. Add the olives, basil and lemon zest. Toss until coated. Add the reserved liquid gradually until the pasta is moist. Chill, covered, until serving time. Serve chilled.

Serves 8

Louisiana Mexican Salad

The Junior Auxiliary of Abbeville, Louisiana, submitted the following recipe. The JA of Abbeville supports various parish nursing homes each year with the Nightingales Project.

1 pound lean ground beef
2 (15-ounce) cans ranch-style beans
2 (10-ounce) packages small
  corn chips, crushed
1 head lettuce, chopped
2 large tomatoes, chopped
2 avocados, chopped

4 cups sour cream
1 (8-ounce) package shredded
  Mexican jalapeño chile
  cheese blend
1 (16-ounce) bottle
  Catalina salad dressing

Brown the ground beef with the beans in a skillet, stirring until the ground beef is crumbly; drain. Layer the corn chips, lettuce, tomatoes, avocados, sour cream and cheese in a large serving bowl. Add the ground beef and salad dressing just before serving and toss until mixed well.

Serves 15

Carolina Fried Chicken Salad

Ninety of Arkansas' most attractive and capable gals donned their new fall suits and bonnets and trekked to Helena . . . for an all-day [Regional] meeting with dinner on the ground. It was during the gossip half-hour that debate ensued over which chapter was the first to persuade the local governments to introduce fluoride into the cities' drinking water. Almost every chapter sponsored a dental clinic in their community.

—NAJA Crownlet, 1955

The Junior Auxiliary of Crystal Springs, Mississippi, donated the following recipe. The JA of Crystal Springs' project, Angel Tree, *organizes the community to deliver gifts to needy children at Christmas.*

Dressing
1 cup vegetable oil
1/3 cup sugar
1/4 cup orange juice
3 tablespoons lemon juice
1 tablespoon apple cider vinegar
1 teaspoon paprika
1 teaspoon onion powder
1 teaspoon salt

Salad
1/4 cup (1/2 stick) butter
1 (2-ounce) package
    chopped pecans

1 tablespoon sugar
1 teaspoon salt
2 pounds boneless skinless chicken
    breasts, coarsely chopped
1/2 cup buttermilk
1 cup all-purpose flour
1/2 cup cornmeal
1 teaspoon salt
1 teaspoon pepper
Vegetable oil for frying
3 (8-ounce) packages salad greens
    (three different types)
1 pound bacon, crisp-cooked and
    crumbled

To prepare the dressing, combine the oil, sugar, orange juice, lemon juice, vinegar, paprika, onion powder and salt in a jar with a tight-fitting lid and seal tightly. Shake to mix. Chill for 24 hours or until serving time. Shake well and allow to come to room temperature before serving.

To prepare the salad, melt the butter in a skillet over low heat. Add the pecans, sugar and 1 teaspoon salt. Cook for 10 minutes, stirring frequently. Drain and break the pecans into pieces. Soak the chicken in the buttermilk in a bowl. Mix the flour, cornmeal, 1 teaspoon salt and the pepper in a bowl. Drain the chicken, discarding the buttermilk. Toss the chicken in the flour mixture until coated. Fry in batches in hot oil in a heavy skillet over medium heat until cooked through; drain. Combine the lettuce, bacon, pecans and hot chicken in a bowl. Add a generous amount of dressing and toss until coated. Serve immediately.

Serves 4 to 6

Chinese Chicken Slaw

DRESSING

1 cup olive oil

1 seasoning packet from chicken-flavor ramen noodles

2 teaspoons salt

1 teaspoon black pepper

1/2 teaspoon garlic powder

1/2 teaspoon onion powder

1/4 teaspoon celery salt

1/4 teaspoon cracked red pepper

SLAW

2 (10-ounce) packages coleslaw mix

2 (3-ounce) packages chicken-flavor ramen noodles

4 to 6 green onions, chopped

3 ribs celery, chopped

1/2 bell pepper, chopped

1 (2-ounce) package slivered almonds

2 boneless skinless chicken breasts, cooked and chopped

To prepare the dressing, mix the olive oil, contents of the seasoning packet, salt, black pepper, garlic powder, onion powder, celery salt and red pepper in a bowl until blended.

To prepare the slaw, combine the coleslaw mix, ramen noodles, green onions, celery, bell pepper, almonds and chicken in a large bowl. Add the dressing and toss until coated. Chill, covered, until serving time.

For a lower-fat dressing, dissolve the contents of the seasoning packet in 2 tablespoons hot water in a bowl. Add 1/2 cup pineapple juice, 5 teaspoons dark sesame oil, 1/2 cup apple cider vinegar, 3 tablespoons sugar, 1/2 teaspoon garlic powder, 1/2 teaspoon onion powder, 1/4 teaspoon celery salt and 1/4 teaspoon red pepper. Whisk until blended.

SERVES 6 TO 8

DELTA WATER

On her first visit to the Greenville, Mississippi, headquarters of NAJA, the JA member came with her mother. Seeing the water in the hotel bathroom, they decided the room was not clean and requested a change, and then another. Finally, in the third bathroom, they noticed a small sign explaining that the water of Greenville contains unique natural mineral deposits, tinting it brown. Thereafter, instructions for first-time NAJA representatives attending headquarters included an explanation of "Delta water."

Chicken Salad Supreme

POPPY SEED DRESSING
1/4 cup honey
1/2 cup apple cider vinegar
2 tablespoons poppy seeds
2 tablespoons mustard
1/4 teaspoon salt
1 cup vegetable oil

SALAD
1/2 cup mayonnaise
1/2 cup whipped cream
1 teaspoon minced onion
1 teaspoon salt
2 1/2 cups finely chopped cooked chicken
1 cup seedless grapes
1 cup chopped pecans or walnuts
1 (3-ounce) can diced pineapple, drained
Lettuce leaves

To prepare the dressing, whisk the honey, vinegar, poppy seeds, mustard and salt in a bowl until blended. Add the oil gradually, whisking constantly until blended.

To prepare the salad, mix 1/4 cup of the dressing, the mayonnaise, whipped cream, onion and salt in a bowl. Fold in the chicken, grapes, pecans and pineapple. Chill, covered, until serving time. Serve over lettuce. Garnish with olives and sweet pickles.

SERVES 6

Cranberry Chicken Salad

CHUTNEY DRESSING
1 (9-ounce) jar chutney
1/2 cup mayonnaise
2 garlic cloves, finely chopped
1/4 teaspoon red pepper flakes

SALAD
2 boneless skinless chicken breasts, cooked and chopped
16 ounces broccoli, chopped
4 green onions, chopped
1 red bell pepper, chopped
1 cup sweetened dried cranberries
1/2 cup peanuts (optional)

To prepare the dressing, mix the chutney, mayonnaise, garlic and red pepper flakes in a bowl. Chill until serving time.

To prepare the salad, combine the chicken, broccoli, green onions, bell pepper and cranberries in a bowl. Add the dressing and toss until coated. Chill, covered, for 1 hour. Sprinkle with the peanuts just before serving.

SERVES 4 TO 6

Chicken Artichoke Pasta Salad

The Junior Auxiliary of Cleveland, Mississippi, contributed this recipe. The JA of Cleveland received the Martha Wise Award in 2001 for Voices of Youth, A Child's Dream *and in 2006 for* Reality Checks, *a project to teach financial responsibility to teens.*

3 to 4 pounds boneless skinless
   chicken breasts
1 envelope fajita seasoning mix
1/4 cup water
8 ounces bow tie pasta
8 ounces penne
2 (16-ounce) packages
   cheese tortellini
1 (14-ounce) jar artichokes
1 (6-ounce) jar
   marinated artichokes

1 (2-ounce) jar pimento
1 (5-ounce) can mushrooms
1 (2-ounce) can sliced black olives
10 green onions, chopped
3/4 cup olive oil
1/2 cup (2 ounces) grated
   Parmesan cheese
1/2 cup fresh parsley, chopped
3 tablespoons balsamic vinegar
1 tablespoon salt
1 tablespoon pepper

Place the chicken in a baking dish. Mix the fajita seasoning mix and water in a bowl. Pour over the chicken. Bake, covered with foil, at 350 degrees for 1 hour or until cooked through. Let stand until cool; drain. Chop the chicken. Cook the pasta according to the package directions. Chop the artichokes in a food processor, if desired. Combine the chicken, pasta, artichokes, marinated artichokes, pimento, mushrooms, olives and green onions in a bowl. Add the olive oil, cheese, parsley, vinegar, salt and pepper. Toss until combined. Let stand to allow the flavors to blend.

Serves 20

Shrimp and Pasta Salad

DRESSING
1/2 cup light olive oil
3 tablespoons Greek seasoning
3 tablespoons fresh lemon juice
3 tablespoons mayonnaise

SALAD
12 ounces small pasta shells
2 pounds peeled cooked shrimp
6 green onions, thinly sliced
1/2 cup chopped fresh basil
1 tablespoon grated lemon zest
1/2 teaspoon crushed red pepper

To prepare the dressing, whisk the olive oil, Greek seasoning, lemon juice and mayonnaise in a bowl until blended.

To prepare the salad, cook the pasta according to the package directions. Combine the pasta, shrimp, green onions, basil, lemon zest and crushed red pepper in a serving bowl. Add the dressing and toss until coated. Serve immediately or chill, covered, for up to 2 days.

SERVES 6 TO 8

Sun-Dried Tomato Tortellini Salad

16 ounces cheese-filled tortellini
8 ounces oil-pack sun-dried
   tomatoes
1/3 cup olive oil
1 tablespoon fresh lemon juice
2 garlic cloves, minced

1 tablespoon freshly ground pepper
1/2 teaspoon salt
8 ounces marinated artichoke
   hearts, drained
4 ounces whole cashews

Cook the pasta according to the package directions. Drain the sun-dried tomatoes, reserving 1 tablespoon of the oil. Chop the tomatoes. Mix the reserved oil, olive oil, lemon juice, garlic, pepper and salt in a bowl. Add the pasta, tomatoes, artichokes and cashews. Toss until coated. Let stand at room temperature for 1 hour to allow the flavors to blend, or chill, covered, for 8 to 10 hours.

SERVES 8

"Upon receiving a NAJA committee appointment, I took my first trip to Greenville. I was enjoying meeting new people and visiting when the chairman received a call, 'It's your husband.' I had completely forgotten to call to let my family know I had arrived safely. After failing to get me on my phone, they alerted the highway patrol. Now when I attend a NAJA event, everyone asks if I have called my family."

—AMY PINKSTON

Honey Poppy Seed Dressing

This recipe is a favorite of the Junior Auxiliary of Wayne County, Mississippi. MRS. MCDONALD'S CLASSROOM *is the JA of Wayne County's project to stock household essentials in a life skills classroom at the local high school.*

1 cup vegetable oil	6 tablespoons poppy seeds
3/4 cup honey	1 1/2 teaspoons salt
6 tablespoons apple cider vinegar	

Combine the oil, honey, vinegar, poppy seeds and salt in a jar with a tight-fitting lid and seal tightly. Shake to mix. Chill until serving time. Serve with fresh fruit.

MAKES 2 CUPS

Chilled Strawberry Soup

2 quarts strawberries	Grated zest of 1 lemon
1 cup sugar	Grated zest of 1 orange
2 cups water	Juice of 1 lemon
2 cups Rhine or moselle wine	(about 3 tablespoons)
(semisweet white wine)	Sour cream

Process the strawberries in a food processor until puréed. Press through a fine mesh strainer into a bowl. Chill until cold. Combine the sugar and water in a 1-quart saucepan. Cook over low heat until the sugar is dissolved, stirring constantly. Bring to a boil. Boil for 10 minutes or until a thin syrup forms. Chill until cold. Mix the strawberry purée, sugar syrup, wine, lemon zest, orange zest and lemon juice in a large bowl. Chill, covered, for 2 to 3 hours to allow the flavors to blend or until serving time. Ladle into chilled cups or bowls. Add a generous dollop of sour cream to each serving. Do not stir in the sour cream. The soup is best when a small amount of the sour cream is taken with each spoonful.

SERVES 10

Butternut Squash Soup

JA OF TUPELO'S
TEEN CANTEEN

*What we are so proud of,
really, is the children
themselves. They didn't ask
for the canteen—no one
did—and we had
misgivings about it and
what our husbands would
say when we chaperoned
and drove at night alone.
Those boys and girls have
fired us with so much
enthusiasm, we can argue
down ten husbands!*

—NAJA CROWNLET, 1953

*The Junior Auxiliary of Cleveland, Tennessee, submitted this favorite
recipe. The JA of Cleveland's FOLA project provides a teddy bear picnic
for preschoolers in the area schools.*

2 pounds butternut squash
2 carrots, sliced
2 ribs celery with leaves, chopped
2 leek bulbs, sliced
1/4 cup (1/2 stick) butter
2 (14-ounce) cans chicken broth
1/2 teaspoon ginger
1/2 cup half-and-half
1/2 teaspoon salt
1/4 teaspoon pepper
1/2 cup chopped pecans, toasted (optional)

Place the squash on a baking sheet. Bake at 350 degrees for 1 hour. Let stand
until slightly cool. Peel, seed and chop the squash. Sauté the carrots, celery and
leeks in the butter in a large saucepan for 10 minutes. Stir in the squash,
broth and ginger. Bring to a boil. Reduce the heat and simmer, covered, for
25 minutes or until the squash is tender. Let stand until lukewarm. Process in
batches in a blender or food processor until smooth; return to the saucepan. Stir in
the half-and-half, salt and pepper. Cook until heated through, stirring occasionally.
Do not bring to a boil. Ladle into serving bowls and sprinkle with the pecans.

SERVES 8

Corn Chowder

This recipe is from the Junior Auxiliary of Tupelo, Mississippi. The JA of Tupelo directs and staffs a one-week summer day camp for girls in the SPECIAL EDITION *project.*

8 ounces kielbasa
1 onion, chopped
4 ribs celery with leaves, chopped
2 tablespoons unsalted butter
2 pounds red potatoes, chopped
8 cups (or more) chicken stock or water
24 ounces frozen Shoe Peg corn, or
    kernels of 5 ears of corn
4 cups half-and-half
1/4 cup (1/2 stick) unsalted butter
1/2 cup all-purpose flour
Salt and pepper to taste
1/2 cup chopped fresh parsley, or fried tortilla strips

Sauté the sausage, onion and celery in 2 tablespoons butter in a large heavy saucepan until tender. Add the potatoes and enough stock to cover. Simmer, covered, for 8 to 10 minutes. Stir in the corn. Simmer, covered, for 10 minutes. Stir in the half-and-half and bring almost to a boil. Melt 1/4 cup butter in a small saucepan. Add the flour and cook until smooth, stirring constantly. Whisk into the corn mixture. Cook over medium-high heat until thickened, stirring frequently. Season with salt and pepper. Sprinkle with the parsley just before serving.

SERVES 8

Tomato Basil Soup

WHAT IS JA?

Junior Auxiliary is Caring
Enough about the children . . .
to work to try to ensure better
Character for Tomorrow . . .

WHAT WILL YOU GET OUT
OF JUNIOR AUXILIARY?

A deep gratification in
knowing that you have had
a part in the tremendous
benefits derived by your
community. The thrill and
satisfaction of making this
world a better place to live.
—NAJA BROCHURE, 1963

1 large sweet onion, chopped
1 cup finely chopped carrots
1 cup finely chopped celery
Butter
3 (14-ounce) cans petite diced tomatoes
1 (14-ounce) can chicken broth
1 tablespoon sugar
2 teaspoons parsley flakes, or 2 tablespoons chopped fresh parsley
1 teaspoon dried basil, or 1 tablespoon chopped fresh basil
1 teaspoon thyme
1 bay leaf
2 tablespoons vegetable oil
1/4 cup all-purpose flour
1 (12-ounce) can evaporated milk
1/2 cup heavy cream
1 teaspoon pepper
2 teaspoons salt

Sauté the onion, carrots and celery in butter in a large saucepan until tender. Add the tomatoes, broth, sugar, parsley, basil, thyme and bay leaf. Simmer for 30 minutes, stirring occasionally. Remove from the heat and let stand to cool for 15 minutes. Discard the bay leaf. Process in batches in a blender or food processor until puréed. Heat the oil in a large saucepan. Add the flour and stir until smooth. Add the evaporated milk and cream gradually, stirring until blended. Cook until thickened, stirring constantly. Stir in the tomato mixture, salt and pepper. Cook until heated through, stirring occasionally. Serve immediately or simmer over low heat until serving time. Garnish with a dollop of sour cream and chopped fresh herbs.

SERVES 6

French Onion Soup

3 tablespoons margarine
1 tablespoon vegetable oil
5 cups thinly sliced yellow onions
1 teaspoon salt
1/4 teaspoon sugar
3 tablespoons all-purpose flour

8 cups beef stock
1/2 cup dry white wine
Salt and pepper to taste
3 tablespoons brandy (optional)
Toasted slices of French bread
Grated Parmesan cheese

Combine the margarine and oil in a large skillet. Add the onions and cook, covered, for 15 minutes. Add the salt and sugar. Cook, uncovered, for 40 minutes or until golden brown, stirring frequently. Stir in the flour. Cook for 3 minutes, stirring frequently. Bring the stock to a boil in a saucepan. Remove the onions from the heat. Add the stock gradually, stirring after each addition. Stir in the wine. Season with salt and pepper. Simmer, partially covered, for 40 minutes, skimming the top as needed. Stir in the brandy just before serving. Ladle into soup bowls. Top with a slice of bread and cheese.

SERVES 6 TO 8

Cheesy Potato Soup

1 (28-ounce) package frozen hash
  brown potatoes
2 teaspoons chicken bouillon
4 cups water
1 pound bacon, crisp-cooked and
  crumbled
1 onion, chopped
1 cup frozen sliced carrots

2 cups sour cream
1/2 cup (1 stick) margarine
2 cups milk
1 teaspoon salt
1/2 teaspoon pepper
8 ounces Velveeta cheese,
  cut into cubes

Combine the potatoes, bouillon and water in a large saucepan. Cook, covered, until the potatoes are thawed. Add the bacon, onion, carrots, sour cream, margarine, milk, salt and pepper; mix well. Stir in the cheese. Cook for 45 minutes or until the carrots are tender, stirring occasionally.

SERVES 8

Old-Fashioned Vegetable Beef Soup

1 pound bone-in steak
Salt and pepper to taste
1/4 cup chopped onion
1/4 cup chopped bell pepper
2 tablespoons olive oil
2 (14-ounce) cans stewed tomatoes
2 (15-ounce) cans tomato sauce
1 chicken bouillon cube

2 beef bouillon cubes
12 to 16 cups water
1/4 small head cabbage, sliced
3 carrots, sliced
1 (15-ounce) can whole kernel corn
4 potatoes, chopped
1 (6-ounce) package spaghetti

Trim and chop the steak into cubes, reserving the bone. Season with salt and pepper. Brown the steak, steak bone, onion and bell pepper in the olive oil in a large heavy saucepan. Add the tomatoes, tomato sauce, chicken bouillon, beef bouillon and water. Bring to a boil. Reduce the heat and simmer for 1 hour. Remove and discard the bone. Add the cabbage, carrots, corn and potatoes. Bring to a gentle boil and cook for 20 minutes. Add the spaghetti and cook for 10 minutes or until the vegetables and spaghetti are tender.

SERVES 6

Creamy Taco Soup

This recipe is from the Junior Auxiliary of Mountain Home, Arkansas. The JA of Mountain Home's project, BABY BUNDLES, *supplies a bathtub with baby necessities for needy mothers.*

1 pound ground beef
1 small onion, diced
1 envelope taco seasoning mix
1 (15-ounce) can pinto beans
1 (15-ounce) can red kidney beans

1 (15-ounce) can whole kernel corn
1 (14-ounce) can diced tomatoes
1 (14-ounce) can beef broth
8 ounces cream cheese, softened

Brown the ground beef with the onion in a large saucepan, stirring until the ground beef is crumbly; drain. Add the taco seasoning mix, pinto beans, kidney beans, corn, tomatoes and broth. Simmer for 45 minutes, stirring occasionally. Add the cream cheese and stir until melted. Remove from the heat. Serve with corn chips.

SERVES 6 TO 8

Male Chauvinist Chili

3 slices bacon, finely chopped
8 ounces Italian sausage, cut into
   1-inch pieces
8 ounces ground beef
2 onions, chopped
1 small green bell pepper, chopped
2 garlic cloves, minced
1 jalapeño chile, chopped

2 (16-ounce) cans crushed Italian-
   style tomatoes
1 (16-ounce) can pinto beans
1 (16-ounce) can garbanzo beans
2 teaspoons Worcestershire sauce
1 tablespoon chili powder
1/2 teaspoon dry mustard
1/4 teaspoon pepper

Sauté the bacon in a skillet until crisp; drain. Brown the sausage and ground beef with the onions in the skillet, stirring until the ground beef is crumbly; drain. Combine the bacon, sausage mixture, bell pepper, garlic and jalapeño chile in a slow cooker. Stir in the tomatoes, pinto beans, garbanzo beans, Worcestershire sauce, chili powder, dry mustard and pepper. Cook on Low for 6 to 14 hours.

SERVES 6 TO 8

White Chicken Chili

The Junior Auxiliary of Clarksville, Arkansas, contributed this recipe. The JA of Clarksville assembles and distributes Christmas and Easter baskets for foster children in the LORRE'S KIDS *project.*

3 or 4 boneless skinless
   chicken breasts
1 onion, chopped (optional)
2 (15-ounce) cans Great
   Northern beans
1 (4-ounce) can diced green chiles
2 cups (8 ounces) shredded
   Monterey Jack and Cheddar
   cheese blend
1 1/2 cups chicken broth

1 cup water
1 teaspoon garlic powder
2 teaspoons cumin
1 teaspoon oregano
1 1/2 teaspoons cayenne pepper
1/2 teaspoon salt
1 cup (4 ounces) shredded
   Monterey Jack and Cheddar
   cheese blend

Cook the chicken in boiling water in a saucepan until cooked through. Reserve 2 1/2 cups of the cooking liquid to use instead of the chicken broth and water, if desired. Shred the chicken and place in a large saucepan. Add the onion, beans, green chiles, 2 cups cheese, broth, water, garlic powder, cumin, oregano, cayenne pepper and salt. Cook for 1 hour, stirring occasionally. Ladle into soup bowls and top each serving with some of the remaining 1 cup cheese.

SERVES 6 TO 8

Southwest Chicken Soup

The bell had rung, and

school was out

Auxiliary members jumped

all about . . .

But, the presidents said,

"It's plain to see,

The Story Hour

is a necessity.

Rest Home visits are made

the year 'round,

Auxiliary members never go

with a frown . . .

Crippled Children's Clinic

you will recall,

Gives the most satisfied

feeling of all."

Now . . . summer's over,

the school bell has rung

Our dreams of vacation,

were surely far flung.

—THE CROWNLET, 1966

1 cup chopped onion
1/2 cup chopped celery
1 tablespoon olive oil
6 cups chicken stock
4 chicken breasts
4 chicken thighs
1/2 cup brown rice
1 (15-ounce) can diced tomatoes
1 (10-ounce) package frozen corn kernels
1 (4-ounce) can chopped green chiles
1 teaspoon cumin
1 tablespoon chili powder
2 tablespoons picante sauce

Sauté the onion and celery in the olive oil in a large stockpot until tender. Stir in the stock, chicken and brown rice. Bring to a boil. Reduce the heat and simmer for 20 to 30 minutes or until the chicken is cooked through and tender. Remove the chicken with a slotted spoon and let stand until cool. Chop the chicken, discarding the bones. Chill, covered, until ready to use.

Chill the soup, covered, for 8 to 10 hours or until the fat rises to the top and hardens. Skim off and discard the fat. Add the chicken, tomatoes, corn, green chiles, cumin, chili powder and picante sauce. Cook until heated through and adjust seasonings to taste.

SERVES 8

Duck Gumbo

5 ducks
1 pound ham hocks
1 onion, quartered
1 bunch celery, chopped
2 tablespoons Creole seasoning
1 tablespoon browning and
  seasoning sauce
6 bay leaves
12 cups water
1/2 cup vegetable oil
1/2 cup all-purpose flour
5 onions, quartered

4 cups okra, chopped
4 cups whole tomatoes
1 green bell pepper, chopped
1 pound smoked sausage, sliced
2 (or more) garlic cloves, minced
1 cup green onion tops, chopped
1 cup parsley, chopped
1/4 cup gumbo filé powder
1 tablespoon cayenne pepper
Tabasco sauce to taste
Hot cooked rice

Combine the ducks, ham hocks, 1 onion, 1 rib of the celery, the Creole seasoning, browning and seasoning sauce and bay leaves in a large stockpot. Add the water. Bring to a boil. Boil until the ducks are tender and cooked through. Skim the surface, removing any fat or impurities. Cook for 30 minutes longer, skimming as needed. Remove the ducks. Chop the meat, discarding the bones. Return the meat to the stock.

Mix the oil and flour in a small saucepan. Cook over medium heat until smooth and deep brown, stirring constantly. Stir into the stock. Add the remaining celery, 5 onions, the okra, tomatoes, bell pepper, sausage and garlic. Cook, covered, over low heat for 4 hours, stirring occasionally and adding more water as needed to cover the vegetables and meat. Remove from the heat. Remove the bay leaves. Stir in the green onions, parsley, gumbo filé powder, cayenne pepper and Tabasco sauce. Serve over hot cooked rice.

SERVES 12

Seafood Gumbo

AWARD WINNER: OH
BABY!—JA OF LAUREL

*Baby Think It Over is an
"infant simulator" designed
to help a potential parent
understand what it's like to
be the primary caregiver of
a baby. Baby Think It Over
does not wet or soil diapers
and does not laugh, smile,
or coo when it is happy. The
only form of feedback it can
give is crying. When the baby
cries, it is the caregiver's job
to determine what type of
care it needs and provide it
quickly, day or night!*

1/2 cup bacon drippings or
   olive oil
1/2 cup all-purpose flour
1 large onion, chopped
1 bell pepper, chopped
3 or 4 ribs celery, chopped
1 (15-ounce) can diced tomatoes
8 ounces okra, sliced
5 cups chicken broth
8 ounces smoked sausage
1 pound shrimp, peeled
1 pound fresh crab claw meat
1 tablespoon minced garlic

1 tablespoon chopped parsley
1 tablespoon Worcestershire sauce
1 tablespoon Old Bay seasoning
1 tablespoon Nature's Seasons
   seasoning blend
1 tablespoon Creole seasoning
1 tablespoon thyme
1 tablespoon oregano
1 tablespoon basil
2 bay leaves
Cayenne pepper to taste
2 tablespoon gumbo filé powder
Hot cooked rice

Mix the bacon drippings and the flour in a large saucepan. Cook over medium
to medium-high heat until the roux is the color of a chocolate bar, stirring
constantly. Add the onion, bell pepper, celery, tomatoes and okra. Stir in the
broth. Add the sausage, shrimp, crab meat, garlic, parsley, Worcestershire sauce,
Old Bay seasoning, Nature's Seasons seasoning blend, Creole seasoning, thyme,
oregano, basil and bay leaves. Season with cayenne pepper. Simmer for 4 hours.
Stir in the gumbo filé powder just before serving. Discard the bay leaves. Serve
over hot cooked rice.

For a variation, substitute fresh crab claws for the crab meat. Fold into the gumbo
just before serving. Fresh crab claws also can be used as a garnish.

SERVES 4 TO 6

Shrimp and Corn Chowder

The Junior Auxiliary of Laurel, Mississippi, chose this recipe as a favorite.
The JA of Laurel is a charter chapter of NAJA, a member since 1941.

12 slices bacon, chopped
2 onions, chopped
$1/2$ cup plus 1 tablespoon all-purpose flour
3 pounds red potatoes, cut into $1/2$-inch pieces (about 9 cups)
6 cups whipping cream
3 (14-ounce) cans chicken broth
3 (15-ounce) cans whole kernel corn, drained
3 tablespoons fresh thyme, or 1 tablespoon dried thyme
$2 1/2$ teaspoons salt
$1 1/2$ teaspoons pepper
3 pounds shrimp, peeled, deveined and chopped

Cook the bacon in a 10-quart saucepan over medium heat until crisp. Remove to paper towels with a slotted spoon, reserving 3 tablespoons of the drippings. Add the onions and cook for 5 minutes or until tender, stirring occasionally. Stir in the flour. Stir in the potatoes, whipping cream, broth, corn, thyme, salt and pepper. Bring to a boil, stirring constantly. Reduce the heat and simmer, partially covered, for 20 minutes or until the potatoes are tender, stirring occasionally. Add the shrimp and simmer until the shrimp turn pink. Ladle into soup bowls and sprinkle with the bacon. Serve immediately.

SERVES 8

Side Dishes & Pasta

Why JA Is So Important

Why is JA so important? Because JA looks for those places others have not gone. JA explores the gaps; it looks for the children who have fallen through the cracks, perhaps because their needs do not fit into a specific category. JA looks for the forgotten child, the forgotten mother, the forgotten senior. JA looks for the forgotten life and says, "You matter."

That's why it is so important for JA chapters to adhere to the JA objective of creating their own projects, independent of the large umbrella organizations. Those organizations are important and do wonderful work—but there are so many needs that do not fall under those broad umbrellas. There are so many children out there who need someone to care, someone to help, someone to go beyond their own comfort zone and reach out to them, to be hands-on with them and show them a better way. ➤

As a member of Junior Auxiliary, the difference you make in a child's life will surely make a difference in your own. You have been blessed; share that blessing. In doing so, you will not only be making a critical difference in another child's life, you will also be setting the most wonderful example for your own children or children that you work with, who will surely be encouraged to carry on the torch of love, kindness, and generosity.

We live in a world that challenges those ideals; Junior Auxiliary provides a way to keep caring alive. What a privilege it is to be involved, and I, for one, am grateful to every individual involved in Junior Auxiliary. It is a great work that you do. Keep it up!

Sesame Asparagus

2 tablespoons sesame seeds
1¹/₂ to 2 pounds thin
   asparagus spears
1¹/₂ tablespoons peanut oil or
   canola oil

1 tablespoon soy sauce
Garlic salt to taste
Pepper to taste
1 tablespoon sesame oil

Cook the sesame seeds in a dry skillet over medium heat until the seeds turn light golden brown and begin to pop, stirring constantly. Remove immediately to a bowl and set aside.

Snap off the woody ends of the asparagus spears. Heat the peanut oil in a skillet over medium heat. Add the asparagus spears and turn gently in the oil to coat. Drizzle with the soy sauce. Season with garlic salt and pepper. Cook, covered, until the asparagus spears are tender-crisp, turning occasionally. Remove from the heat. Drizzle with the sesame oil and sprinkle with the sesame seeds. Toss until coated.

SERVES 6 TO 8

Baked Green Beans

The Junior Auxiliary of Amory, Mississippi, submitted this recipe from their cookbook, LOOK WHO CAME TO DINNER. *The JA of Amory was selected in 2000 for the Martha Wise Award for the* I.H.U.G. (I HAVE UNIQUE GIFTS) PROJECT *and the Louise Eskrigge Crump Award for the* M&Ms (MENTOR MOMS) PROJECT.

1 cup packed brown sugar
¹/₂ cup apple cider vinegar
1 teaspoon dry mustard
1 pinch of seasoning salt

3 (14-ounce) cans green
   beans, drained
Chopped onion to taste
3 or 4 slices bacon
Seasoning salt to taste

Mix the brown sugar, vinegar, dry mustard and 1 pinch of seasoning salt in a saucepan. Bring to a boil, stirring occasionally. Layer half the green beans, the onion, remaining green beans and the bacon in a baking dish. Sprinkle with additional seasoning salt. Pour the brown sugar mixture over the top. Bake, covered, at 300 degrees for 1 hour.

SERVES 8

"The last duty of an Active member is to write a letter requesting to go Associate. My provisional class chose to meet at a local restaurant, reminisce about the past five and a half years, and then compose our letters. As I sat there listening, laughing, and eating, I found I just couldn't write the letter that would end my years of Active service to an organization I truly loved. Instead, I requested to remain an Associate-Active member, a status I held for several more years."

—SHARON HUDSON

Sweet-and-Sour Green Beans

2 (or more) slices bacon
3 tablespoons dark brown sugar
1 teaspoon mustard
2 tablespoons apple cider vinegar
2 (16-ounce) cans French-style green beans, drained
2 tablespoons minced green onions

Cook the bacon in a skillet until crisp; drain, reserving 1/4 cup of the drippings. Crumble the bacon and set aside. Add the brown sugar, mustard and vinegar to the reserved drippings. Simmer for 3 minutes, stirring occasionally. Cook the green beans in a saucepan until heated through. Fold in the green onions. Add the brown sugar mixture and toss until coated. Sprinkle with the bacon and serve immediately.

SERVES 8

Green Beans with Almonds

1/4 cup slivered almonds
1/4 cup (1/2 stick) margarine
1/4 cup chopped green tomatoes
1/2 teaspoon salt
4 cups hot cooked green beans

Cook the almonds in the margarine in a saucepan over low heat until golden brown, stirring occasionally. Remove from the heat. Stir in the tomatoes and salt. Mix the almond mixture and the green beans in a serving dish. Serve hot.

SERVES 6

Green Bean Mushroom Pie

This recipe is a favorite of the JA of Camden, Arkansas. The JA of Camden provides food, clothing and medical assistance to needy children through the P.A.L.S. project.

FILLING
3 cups sliced mushrooms
1 tablespoon butter
6 cups green beans, cut into
　1-inch pieces
2 1/2 cups chopped onions
3 tablespoons butter
8 ounces cream cheese,
　cut into cubes
1/2 cup milk
2 teaspoons minced fresh thyme, or
　3/4 teaspoon dried thyme
1/2 teaspoon salt
1/4 teaspoon pepper

PASTRY
2 1/2 cups all-purpose flour
2 teaspoons baking powder
1 teaspoon dill weed
1/4 teaspoon salt
1 cup (2 sticks) cold butter,
　cut into pieces
1 cup sour cream
1 egg
1 tablespoon heavy whipping
　cream

To prepare the filling, sauté the mushrooms in 1 tablespoon butter in a skillet until tender; drain. Sauté the green beans and onions in 3 tablespoons butter in the skillet for 18 to 20 minutes or until the green beans are tender-crisp. Add the mushrooms, cream cheese, milk, thyme, salt and pepper. Cook until the cream cheese is melted, stirring constantly. Remove from the heat and set aside.

To prepare the pastry, mix the flour, baking powder, dill weed and salt in a large bowl. Cut in the butter until crumbly. Add the sour cream and stir until a soft dough forms. Divide the dough into two equal portions.

To assemble, roll out one portion of the pastry on a well-floured surface. Fit into a 9-inch pie plate and trim the edge. Spoon the green bean mixture into the pie shell. Roll out the remaining portion of pastry and cut into strips. Arrange lattice-fashion over the pie; trim. Flute the edge to seal. Beat the egg and cream in a small bowl until smooth. Brush over the top of the pie. Bake at 400 degrees for 25 to 35 minutes or until golden brown.

SERVES 8 TO 10

Calico Baked Beans

The Junior Auxiliary of DeSoto County, Mississippi, submitted this recipe. The JA of DeSoto County holds a parents' night out for house parents at the local orphanage through the chapter's project, PALMER HOME ACTIVITY NIGHT.

8 ounces turkey bacon, chopped	1 (15- or 16-ounce) can butter
1 onion, chopped	beans, drained
3/4 cup packed brown sugar	1 (15- or 16-ounce) can lima
3/4 cup ketchup	beans, drained
3 tablespoons vinegar	1 (15- or 16-ounce) can kidney
1 (28-ounce) can baked beans	beans, drained

Cook the bacon and onion in a saucepan until the onion is tender and the bacon is cooked through. Add the brown sugar, ketchup and vinegar; mix well. Stir in the baked beans, butter beans, lima beans and kidney beans. Spoon into a large baking dish. Bake at 350 degrees for 45 to 60 minutes.

SERVES 6 TO 8

Broccoli Corn Bake

PROUD AS A PEACOCK *is the cookbook of the Junior Auxiliary of Savannah, Tennessee. The JA of Savannah conducts an all-night drug- and alcohol-free party for graduating seniors in high school with* PROJECT GRADUATION.

1 (10-ounce) package frozen	1/2 teaspoon salt
chopped broccoli, thawed	1 dash of pepper
1 (16-ounce) can cream-style corn	1/4 cup cracker crumbs
1 egg, beaten	2 tablespoons butter, melted
1 tablespoon dried minced onion	

Mix the broccoli, corn, egg, dried onion, salt and pepper in a bowl. Spoon into a 11/2-quart baking dish. Mix the cracker crumbs and butter in a small bowl and sprinkle over the top. Bake at 350 degrees for 45 minutes.

SERVES 6

"*The most heartwarming thing about being in Junior Auxiliary is knowing that you are working with the best group of caring, committed, and loyal women in our area. It is absolutely amazing to me to look back over the years at the history and the many, many lives that have been directly touched by JA. I count myself truly blessed to be a part of such a fine organization.*"

—ACTIVE MEMBER,
JA OF SAVANNAH

Cabbage, Onion and Bell Pepper Medley

3 tablespoons vinegar, red wine vinegar or balsamic vinegar
1 tablespoon vegetable oil
1 tablespoon water
1 1/2 teaspoons brown sugar
1 1/2 teaspoons Dijon mustard
1/2 teaspoon salt

1/2 teaspoon pepper
2 slices bacon
1 small red bell pepper, sliced
1 small yellow bell pepper, sliced
1 onion, chopped
2 cups shredded cabbage

Combine the vinegar, oil, water, brown sugar, Dijon mustard, salt and pepper in a jar with a tight-fitting lid and seal tightly. Shake to mix. Cook the bacon in a skillet until crisp; drain, reserving the drippings. Crumble the bacon. Cook the bell peppers, onion and cabbage in the reserved drippings in the skillet and toss until coated. Add the dressing. Bring to a boil, stirring occasionally. Reduce the heat and simmer, covered, for 10 minutes or until the vegetables are tender. Sprinkle with the bacon.

SERVES 2 TO 4

Carrot Soufflé

The Junior Auxiliary of New Albany, Mississippi, includes this recipe in the cookbook TALLAHATCHIE'S BEST COOKBOOK. *The JA of New Albany conducts* MUSEUM MADNESS, *a variety of cultural workshops for students at the Union County Museum.*

2 pounds carrots, boiled and mashed
1/2 cup (1 stick) butter, melted
1 cup granulated sugar
3 tablespoons all-purpose flour

1 teaspoon baking powder
1 teaspoon vanilla extract
3 eggs, beaten
Confectioners' sugar

Mix the carrots, butter, granulated sugar, flour, baking powder, vanilla and eggs in a bowl. Spoon into a soufflé dish and dust with confectioners' sugar. Bake at 350 degrees for 30 minutes.

SERVES 6 TO 8

Salad is served at our annual Spaghetti Supper and our members chop the lettuce in large quantities. One year, the member in charge of keeping the salad replenished on the serving line realized about thirty minutes after the last refill that her diamond ring was missing. As the story goes, she was in a state of panic not knowing where it was. After much searching, it was finally found in the serving area. Everyone had feared that a patron would find it and think it was a prize!

—JA OF HOPE

Brandied Cranberries

1 pound cranberries
2 cups sugar
1/4 cup (or more) brandy

Place the cranberries in a medium baking dish. Sprinkle with the sugar. Bake, covered, at 350 degrees for 50 to 60 minutes. Let stand until cool. Drizzle with the brandy.

SERVES 8 TO 10

Italian-Style Eggplant Stacks

The Junior Auxiliary of Pascagoula-Moss Point, Mississippi, submitted this recipe from the cookbook, BOUQUET GARNI. The JA of Pascagoula-Moss Point serves dinner to children in a local outreach program with the HOPE HOUSE project.

1 large eggplant
Salt to taste
3 or 4 tomatoes, sliced
1 large onion, thinly sliced
Pepper to taste
1 to 2 teaspoons chopped basil

1/2 cup (1 stick) butter, melted
6 ounces mozzarella cheese, shredded
1/4 cup (1 ounce) grated Parmesan cheese
1/2 cup bread crumbs

Slice the eggplant 1/2 inch thick and place immediately in salted ice water to soak for 15 minutes; drain. Layer an eggplant slice, tomato slice and onion slice in stacks in a greased 9×13-inch baking dish. Season with salt and pepper. Sprinkle with the basil and drizzle with the butter. Bake at 450 degrees for 20 minutes. Top with the mozzarella cheese, Parmesan cheese and bread crumbs. Bake for 10 minutes longer.

SERVES 6

Baked Okra

This recipe is from the Junior Auxiliary of Harrison, Arkansas. The JA of Harrison provides food for children in the local Headstart Preschool program during long school breaks with the chapter's BACKPACK BUDDIES *project.*

4 slices bacon	1 large onion, chopped
1 pound okra, cut into	1 bell pepper, chopped
1/2-inch slices	3/4 teaspoon salt
1 cup sliced mushrooms	1/8 teaspoon pepper

Cook the bacon in a skillet until crisp; drain, reserving 2 tablespoons of the drippings. Sauté the okra, mushrooms, onion, and bell pepper in the reserved drippings in the skillet until tender. Add the salt and pepper. Spoon into a 9-inch pie plate. Top with the bacon. Bake at 350 degrees for 30 minutes.

SERVES 4

Fried Okra

1 pound okra, sliced	1/2 cup cornmeal
Salt to taste	Shortening or vegetable oil
3 tablespoons all-purpose flour	for frying

Place the okra in a bowl and season with salt. Add the flour and toss until coated. Add the cornmeal and toss until coated. Heat shortening in a deep skillet over medium heat. Fry the okra, in batches if needed, until golden brown; drain. Increase the heat after 15 minutes if needed. Serve immediately.

SERVES 4

Twice-Baked Cottage-Style Potatoes

The Junior Auxiliary of Covington-Tipton County, Tennessee's cookbook, RECIPE RECOLLECTIONS, *includes this recipe. The JA of Covington-Tipton County delivers toys weekly to children in the local hospital through the* LITTLE RED BASKET *project.*

2 baking potatoes
1/2 cup low-fat cottage cheese
2 tablespoons skim milk
2 teaspoons sliced green onions
1/8 teaspoon salt
1/8 teaspoon pepper
1/8 teaspoon paprika

Pierce the potatoes three or four times with a fork. Bake at 400 degrees for 1 hour or until tender. Let stand until cool. Cut the top skin from the potatoes and hollow out to make a shell; set aside. Mash the potato pulp in a bowl. Process the cottage cheese and milk in a blender until smooth. Add to the potato pulp and mix well. Stir in the green onions, salt and pepper. Spoon into the potato shells. Sprinkle with the paprika and place on a baking sheet or in a baking pan. Bake at 400 degrees for 10 minutes or until heated through. Garnish with sprigs of parsley.

SERVES 2

"I like to think of Junior Auxiliary as a pioneering organization—it is not necessarily cast in a rigid mold. It has been—and I hope always will be—a flexible group adjusting to changing conditions and to changing requirements as the times so dictate."

—MARTHA WISE,
NAJA CROWNLET, 1961

Parmesan Potatoes

1/4 cup all-purpose flour
1/2 cup (2 ounces) grated
  Parmesan cheese
Salt and pepper to taste

6 to 8 potatoes, peeled
  and chopped
1/2 cup (1 stick) butter or margarine
Paprika

Mix the flour, cheese, salt and pepper in a clean nonrecycled brown paper bag. Add the potatoes and shake until coated. Melt the butter in a 9×13-inch baking dish. Place the potatoes on their side in the butter in the baking dish. Sprinkle with the remaining flour mixture. Sprinkle with paprika. Bake at 350 degrees for 1 hour. Do not turn the potatoes during cooking.

Serves 6

Sweet Potato Casserole

This recipe is from the Junior Auxiliary of Yazoo City, Mississippi. Camp Magnificent Me *is a project of the JA of Yazoo City to host a summer day camp for teen girls to teach self-esteem, etiquette, babysitting, hygiene, and other life skills.*

3 cups mashed cooked sweet
  potatoes
1 cup granulated sugar
2 eggs, lightly beaten
1 teaspoon vanilla extract

1/4 cup heavy cream
1 cup packed brown sugar
1 cup chopped pecans
1/2 cup self-rising flour
1/2 cup (1 stick) butter, melted

Mix the sweet potatoes, granulated sugar, eggs and vanilla in a bowl. Stir in the cream. Spoon into a greased baking dish. Mix the brown sugar, pecans, flour and butter in a bowl with a fork. Crumble over the sweet potato mixture. Bake at 350 degrees for 20 to 30 minutes or until the topping is golden brown. This dish freezes well.

Serves 6 to 8

Spinach Madeline

"The word auxiliary *was chosen for our name because . . . it means to hold as a unit."*

—LOUISE ESKRIGGE CRUMP, SPEAKING AT THE REGION III MEETING ON OCTOBER 5, 1954

4 (10-ounce) packages frozen chopped spinach
1/2 cup (1 stick) butter
1/4 cup all-purpose flour
1/4 cup chopped onion
1 cup evaporated milk
1 1/2 teaspoons minced garlic
1 1/2 teaspoons celery salt
1 teaspoon Worcestershire sauce
1 teaspoon black pepper
1/2 teaspoon salt
Cayenne pepper to taste
2 (6-ounce) rolls jalapeño chile processed cheese, chopped
1 cup bread crumbs or cracker crumbs

Cook the spinach according to the package directions; drain, reserving 1 cup of the cooking liquid. Melt the butter in a large skillet. Add the flour gradually, stirring constantly until blended and smooth. Do not brown. Add the onion and cook until tender, stirring constantly. Add the reserved cooking liquid gradually, stirring constantly until blended and thickened. Add the evaporated milk, garlic, celery salt, Worcestershire sauce, black pepper, salt, cayenne pepper and cheese. Cook until the cheese is melted, stirring constantly. Stir in the spinach.

Spoon into a 9×11-inch baking dish and sprinkle with the bread crumbs. Bake at 350 degrees for 30 minutes. This dish can be made ahead of time and chilled, covered, for up to 24 hours. Add 10 minutes to the baking time.

SERVES 10 TO 12

Two-Cheese Squash Casserole

4 pounds yellow squash, sliced
1 large sweet onion, finely chopped
2 garlic cloves, minced
2 tablespoons butter or margarine
1 cup soft bread crumbs
3/4 cup (3 ounces) shredded Parmesan cheese
1 cup (4 ounces) shredded Cheddar cheese
1 cup sour cream
2 eggs, lightly beaten
1/2 cup fresh chives, chopped
1/2 cup fresh parsley, minced
1 teaspoon salt
1 teaspoon freshly ground pepper
1 1/2 cups soft bread crumbs
1/2 cup (2 ounces) grated Parmesan cheese
2 tablespoons butter or margarine, melted
1/4 teaspoon garlic salt

Cook the squash in boiling water in a large saucepan for 8 to 10 minutes or until tender; drain. Press gently between paper towels to remove excess water. Sauté the onion and garlic in 2 tablespoons butter in a skillet over medium-high heat for 5 to 6 minutes or until tender. Remove from the heat and stir in the squash, 1 cup bread crumbs, 3/4 cup Parmesan cheese, the Cheddar cheese, sour cream, eggs, chives, parsley, salt and pepper. Spoon into a 9×13-inch baking dish. Mix 1 1/2 cups bread crumbs, 1/2 cup Parmesan cheese, 2 tablespoons melted butter and the garlic salt in a bowl. Sprinkle over the squash mixture. Bake at 350 degrees for 35 to 40 minutes or until firm.

Serves 8 to 10

Fresh Tomato Pie

The Junior Auxiliary of Greenwood, Mississippi, includes this recipe in their cookbook, Delta Delights. *The JA of Greenwood is a charter member of NAJA, a member since 1941.*

Basic Pastry Dough
2 cups sifted all-purpose flour
1 teaspoon salt
1/4 cup cold water
2/3 cup shortening

Filling
4 to 5 tomatoes
8 ounces mozzarella cheese, shredded
2 tablespoons chopped fresh basil
1/2 teaspoon salt
1/4 teaspoon pepper
1/4 cup extra-virgin olive oil

To prepare the pastry dough, sift the flour with the salt. Mix one-third of the flour mixture with the water in a bowl. This will form a paste. Cut the shortening into the remaining flour until crumbly. Stir into the paste. Divide the pastry dough into two portions. Shape each into a ball; flatten slightly. Chill, covered, until cold. Roll out one portion on a floured surface. Fit into a 10-inch springform pan. Reserve the remaining pastry dough for another use.

To prepare the filling, cut the tomatoes into 1/2-inch slices. Layer the cheese, half the basil, the tomatoes, salt, pepper, olive oil and remaining basil in the pie shell. Bake at 400 degrees for 30 to 40 minutes. Serve warm.

Serves 8 to 10

Goat Cheese Grits

3 1/2 cups water
1 cup quick-cooking grits
1/2 teaspoon salt

1/2 cup whipping cream
6 ounces goat cheese, crumbled

Bring the water to a boil in a large saucepan. Add the grits gradually, stirring until blended. Add the salt. Bring to a boil. Reduce the heat and stir in the cream gradually. Simmer, covered, for 5 minutes, stirring occasionally. Remove from the heat and add the cheese, stirring until melted. Serve hot.

Serves 6

Hot Tomato Grits

2 slices bacon, chopped
2 (14-ounce) cans ready-to-serve chicken broth
1/2 teaspoon salt
1 cup quick-cooking grits
2 large tomatoes, peeled and chopped
2 tablespoons chopped green chiles
1 cup (4 ounces) shredded Cheddar cheese

Cook the bacon in a skillet until crisp. Add the broth gradually. Add the salt
and bring to a boil. Add the grits gradually, stirring until mixed well. Stir in
the tomatoes and green chiles. Return to a boil, stirring frequently. Reduce
the heat and simmer for 15 to 20 minutes, stirring frequently. Stir in the cheese.
Let stand, covered, for 5 minutes or until the cheese is melted.

SERVES 6

Hominy Casserole

1 onion, chopped
1/2 cup (1 stick) margarine
2 (15-ounce) cans yellow hominy, drained
2 jalapeño chiles, finely chopped
1 (10-ounce) can cream of mushroom soup
3/4 cup (3 ounces) shredded processed cheese
Salt and pepper to taste

Sauté the onion in the margarine in a saucepan until tender. Stir in the hominy,
jalapeño chiles, soup and cheese. Season with salt and pepper. Spoon into a
baking dish. Bake at 350 degrees for 30 minutes.

SERVES 4 TO 6

Cranberry Wild Rice

"At the school for recalcitrant children, Fun Friday was an event for good behavior. I was helping a boy create a pipe cleaner Christmas ornament. He delighted in my attention. Upon finishing, he offered the bracelet to me . . . 'No, it is for someone special.' He insisted and I realized that I was his special person. Through my tears, I gave him a hug. I had come that day to give, but instead, was the recipient."

—ACTIVE MEMBER, JA OF HOT SPRINGS

The Junior Auxiliary of Cabot, Arkansas, donated the following recipe from the chapter's cookbook, TASTEFUL TRADITIONS. *The JA of Cabot won the 2007 Martha Wise Award for* THE WAR AT HOME—FIGHTING CRYSTAL METHAMPHETAMINE *program.*

1/2 cup chopped shallots
1 garlic clove, minced
1/2 cup (1 stick) unsalted butter
1 teaspoon dried thyme
1/2 teaspoon dried sage
1 cup dried cranberries
1/4 cup chicken broth
1 1/2 teaspoons salt
1/2 teaspoon pepper
2 cups wild rice, cooked

Sauté the shallots and garlic in the butter with the thyme and sage in a large skillet over medium heat until tender. Stir in the cranberries, broth, salt and pepper. Bring to a boil and fold in the rice. Spoon into a 3-quart baking dish sprayed with nonstick cooking spray. Bake, covered with foil, at 350 degrees for 20 minutes or until heated through.

SERVES 10 TO 12

Hot Rice

This recipe is from the Junior Auxiliary of Hot Springs, Arkansas. The JA of Hot Springs creates a shopping experience for alternative school students in the chapter's Summit Street Merit Room *project.*

2 cups rice
2 cups chicken broth
1/3 cup creamy Italian salad dressing
1 cup sour cream
2 tablespoons chopped jalapeño chiles
1 tablespoon jalapeño chile juice
1 (8-ounce) can water chestnuts, drained and chopped
2 cups (8 ounces) shredded Monterey Jack cheese

Cook the rice according to the package directions, substituting the broth for the water. Mix the salad dressing, sour cream, jalapeño chiles, jalapeño chile juice and water chestnuts in a bowl. Stir in 1 1/2 cups of the cheese. Fold in the rice. Spoon into a baking dish and sprinkle with the remaining 1/2 cup cheese. Bake at 350 degrees for 30 minutes or until heated through.

Serves 6 to 8

"We were closing the NAJA time capsule at the fiftieth anniversary dinner at the Greenville Country Club. My friend, Catherine, and I sat with a group of people we had not known, but we had such a great time that by the end, we all swore eternal friendship! We signed the menu card, added our fingerprints in lipstick, and pledged that we would all be back in twenty-five years! It turns out that in that group were at least two future NAJA presidents along with several future Regional Directors and chapter presidents."

—MICHELLE HEIDELBERG

Quick Manicotti

8 manicotti shells	1/4 cup mayonnaise
1 pound ground beef	1/2 teaspoon salt
1 garlic clove, crushed	1 (15-ounce) jar spaghetti sauce or
1 cup cottage cheese	tomato sauce
1 cup (4 ounces) shredded	1/2 teaspoon oregano
mozzarella cheese	1/3 cup grated Parmesan cheese

Cook the manicotti shells according to the package directions; drain. Rinse in cold water to stop the cooking process. Brown the ground beef with the garlic in a skillet, stirring until the ground beef is crumbly; drain. Stir in the cottage cheese, mozzarella cheese, mayonnaise and salt. Spoon into the manicotti shells. Place in a lightly greased 9×13-inch baking dish. Mix the spaghetti sauce and oregano in a bowl. Pour over the manicotti. Sprinkle with the Parmesan cheese. Bake, covered, at 350 degrees for 15 minutes. Bake, uncovered, for 10 minutes longer.

SERVES 8

Manicotti Florentine

1 cup tomato sauce or	Salt and pepper to taste
spaghetti sauce	1 (8-ounce) package
1/4 cup water	manicotti shells
1/2 (10-ounce) package frozen	1 cup tomato sauce or
chopped spinach,	spaghetti sauce
thawed and drained	1 cup (4 ounces) shredded
1 cup cottage cheese	mozzarella cheese
1/2 cup ricotta cheese	

Mix 1 cup tomato sauce and the water in a bowl. Spread in a 9×13-inch baking dish. Mix the spinach, cottage cheese and ricotta cheese in a bowl. Season with salt and pepper. Spoon by teaspoonfuls into the pasta shells . Arrange over the tomato sauce mixture. Pour 1 cup tomato sauce over the top. Bake, covered with foil, at 375 degrees for 50 minutes. Sprinkle with the mozzarella cheese. Bake, uncovered, for 10 minutes longer or until the cheese melts. Let stand for 10 to 15 minutes before serving.

SERVES 5

Chicken Lasagna Florentine

The Junior Auxiliary of Columbus, Mississippi, contributed this favorite recipe. The JA of Columbus won the 2007 Norma DeLong Award for In My Shoes, *a project to educate children about disabilities.*

6 lasagna noodles
2 cups chopped cooked chicken
2 cups (8 ounces) shredded Italian cheese blend
16 ounces spinach, cooked, drained and chopped
1 cup chopped mushrooms
1 (10-ounce) can garlic cream of mushroom soup
1/3 cup mayonnaise
1/3 cup finely chopped onion

1 tablespoon cornstarch
1 tablespoon soy sauce
1/2 teaspoon salt
1/4 teaspoon black pepper
1/4 teaspoon freshly grated nutmeg
1 cup (4 ounces) freshly grated Parmesan cheese
2/3 cup chopped pecans
1/4 teaspoon cayenne pepper
1 tablespoon butter, softened

Cook the pasta according to the package directions; drain. Mix the chicken, cheese, spinach, mushrooms, soup, mayonnaise, onion, cornstarch, soy sauce, salt, black pepper and nutmeg in a bowl. Layer the noodles and chicken mixture one-half at a time in a greased 7×11-inch baking dish. Top with the Parmesan cheese. Cook the pecans with the cayenne pepper in the butter in a skillet for 3 minutes, stirring occasionally. Let stand until cool. Sprinkle over the Parmesan cheese. Bake, covered with foil, at 350 degrees for 55 to 60 minutes or until bubbly and heated through. Let stand for 15 minutes before cutting.

SERVES 6 TO 8 SERVINGS

Seafood Lasagna

1 teaspoon minced onion
1 teaspoon minced garlic
1 to 2 teaspoons chopped fresh
    thyme, or to taste
2 to 3 tablespoons olive oil
1/3 cup white wine
1 pound catfish fillets, cooked
    and flaked
1 1/2 pounds shrimp
2 cups water
2 teaspoons celery salt
2 teaspoons salt
2 teaspoons pepper
1 (16-ounce) package
    lasagna noodles

1 1/2 cups feta cheese
1 1/2 cups reduced-fat
    cottage cheese
1/3 cup lemon juice
1 to 2 teaspoons finely chopped
    fresh basil
1/2 teaspoon minced garlic
1/2 teaspoon fennel seeds
2 tablespoons all-purpose flour
1/4 cup milk
1/2 cup (2 ounces) freshly grated
    Parmesan cheese
16 ounces mozzarella cheese,
    shredded
1/2 cup chopped fresh parsley

Sauté the onion and 1 teaspoon garlic with the thyme in the olive oil in a large nonstick skillet over medium-low heat until the onion is tender. Add the wine gradually. Bring to a boil and boil for 1 1/2 minutes. Remove from the heat. Fold in the catfish.

Peel and devein the shrimp, reserving the shells. Mix the shells, water, celery salt, salt and pepper in a small saucepan. Bring to a boil. Boil until the liquid is reduced to 1 2/3 cups. Strain into a large measuring cup, discarding the solids. Add the shrimp to the hot shrimp stock and let stand to cook slightly. Strain, reserving 1 2/3 cups shrimp stock.

Cook the pasta according to the package directions; drain. Mix the feta cheese, cottage cheese, lemon juice, basil, 1/2 teaspoon garlic and the fennel seeds in a bowl; set aside.

Place the flour in a saucepan. Add the milk gradually, whisking until blended. Add the shrimp stock gradually, whisking until blended. Bring to a boil. Reduce the heat and simmer for 5 minutes or until thickened, stirring occasionally. Remove from the heat and stir in the Parmesan cheese.

Layer the Parmesan cheese sauce, pasta, feta cheese mixture, catfish, shrimp and mozzarella cheese one-half at a time in a large lasagna dish sprayed with nonstick cooking spray. Sprinkle with the parsley. Chill, covered, for 8 to 10 hours. Bake, covered, at 350 degrees for 30 minutes. Bake, uncovered, for 30 to 45 minutes longer or until bubbly. Let stand for 15 minutes before serving. This dish freezes well.

Serves 8 to 12

Artichoke Spinach Lasagna

1 onion, chopped
4 garlic cloves, chopped
1 (14-ounce) can vegetable broth or chicken broth
1 teaspoon rosemary
2 (14-ounce) cans artichoke hearts
2 (10-ounce) packages frozen chopped spinach,
   thawed and drained
1 (16-ounce) jar roasted garlic Parmesan cheese pasta sauce
   or Alfredo sauce
9 uncooked lasagna noodles
3 cups (12 ounces) mozzarella cheese
1 (6-ounce) package crumbled feta cheese

Sauté the onion and garlic in a skillet for 3 minutes. Stir in the broth and
rosemary. Bring to a boil. Add the artichoke hearts and spinach. Simmer for
5 minutes. Stir in the pasta sauce and remove from the heat.

Spread a small portion of the artichoke sauce in a 9×13-inch baking dish sprayed
with nonstick cooking spray. Layer the pasta, mozzarella cheese and remaining
artichoke sauce one-third at a time in the prepared dish. Top with the feta cheese.
Bake, covered, at 350 degrees for 40 minutes. Bake, uncovered, for 15 minutes
longer. Let stand for 15 minutes before serving.

Serves 8

Shrimp and Olive Pasta

"Unpaid and often
unappreciated leaders,
Projects, civic, cultural
and financial,
Personal relationships and
families on hold,
Tears, laughter, decades of
stories untold,
Gentle revolutions or skills
of lifetime safety,
Angel encounters and by-
laws drafted,
Courageous women leading
the believers,
Dedicated and passionate
overachievers . . .
Relax; enjoy the tales of
crusades undertaken,
It's only the world you have
molded and shaken . . ."
—Ann Guice, NAJA
President, 1981–1982

1 (16-ounce) package spaghetti, angel hair pasta, elbow pasta
   or bow tie pasta
1 large onion, chopped
1 bunch green onions, chopped
1 pound mushrooms, sliced
2 garlic cloves, chopped
1 handful flat-leaf parsley, chopped
Olive oil
2 pounds peeled medium or large shrimp
2 tablespoons butter
1/2 teaspoon oregano
1 cup heavy cream
1 cup drained sliced black olives
1 cup (4 ounces) shredded mozzarella cheese
1/3 cup Romano cheese

Cook the pasta according to the package directions until al dente; drain. Sauté the onion, green onions, mushrooms and garlic with the parsley in olive oil in a large skillet until the onions are tender. Sauté the shrimp in the butter and olive oil in a skillet. Fold into the onion mixture. Add the oregano. Add the cream gradually, stirring until mixed well. Bring to a simmer and simmer until the shrimp turn pink. Add the pasta and toss until coated. Spoon into an oiled 11/2-quart baking dish. Fold in the olives, mozzarella cheese and Romano cheese. Bake at 275 degrees until heated through.

Serves 8

Linguini with Brie and Shrimp

4 large tomatoes
1 cup fresh basil leaves
8 ounces Brie cheese, rind removed and cheese chopped
3 garlic cloves, minced
1/4 to 1/3 cup olive oil
3/4 teaspoon salt
1/2 teaspoon pepper
16 ounces linguini
8 ounces shrimp, peeled
1 teaspoon shrimp boil
Grated Parmesan cheese

Cut the tomatoes into 1/2-inch pieces. Stack the basil leaves and roll tightly like a cigar. Slice thinly across the stem horitzontally. Mix the tomatoes, chiffonade of basil, Brie cheese, garlic, olive oil, salt and pepper in a large serving bowl. Let stand, covered, at room temperature for 2 hours. Cook the pasta according to the package directions; drain. Cook the shrimp with the shrimp boil in simmering water in a saucepan for 2 to 3 minutes or until the shrimp turn pink; drain. Chop the shrimp and fold into the tomato mixture. Add the hot pasta and toss until coated. Top with Parmesan cheese.

SERVES 4 TO 6

Beef, Pork & Game

Lunch Buddies

Through the years hundreds of children have participated in our Lunch Buddy Program. Nine years ago, Broderick was called out of his fourth grade class to meet Gary, a local banker whose wife was active in the Jonesboro Junior Auxiliary. Broderick's mother had moved away, leaving Broderick to be raised by an aunt and uncle. An outgoing young man, Broderick could hardly wait to introduce Gary to all of his friends. At the end of the school year, Gary promised he would return after the summer break.

Two years later, Broderick was in an accident while visiting his mother. When he returned to Jonesboro, his aunt and uncle sought medical care for him and discovered he needed surgery on one leg. A year later, he had to have surgery on the other leg. During this time, Broderick missed a lot of school. On his own, Broderick may not have received the help he needed to complete his schoolwork. However, Gary continued visiting him at home and insisted that Broderick's teachers send his work home so he would not fall behind in his classes. ➤

Because Broderick could not participate in sports, a junior high coach asked if he would help the team as their manager. Since that time, Broderick has managed the football, basketball, and track teams, even doing a little coaching. He leads the official team prayer and has been a role model to many young athletes. Broderick will graduate this spring with a 3.89 grade point average. He has been involved with choir, band, student council, athletics, and numerous other school clubs. Broderick has also served on community councils and is very active in his church.

Having become very close friends, Broderick is quick to mention life lessons that Gary taught him. Gary always had a way of making Broderick want to try harder. Broderick remembers upon his first meeting with Gary that he was so excited that "someone wants to take time out to come see me." He is "so grateful to God for Gary and so grateful that God sent him into my life at just the right time."

Without Gary and the Junior Auxiliary Lunch Buddies Program, Broderick's life may have taken a different path. Broderick is a shining example of Junior Auxiliary touching one child at a time and forever changing his or her future. Broderick is now in college.

Braised Sirloin Tips with Almond Rice

1 1/2 pounds mushrooms, sliced
1/4 cup (1/2 stick) butter
1 tablespoon olive oil
1 (3-pound) sirloin steak, cut into
   1-inch pieces
3/4 cup beef consommé
3/4 cup red wine
2 tablespoons soy sauce

2 tablespoons cornstarch
1/4 cup beef consommé
1/2 (10-ounce) can cream of
   mushroom soup
Salt to taste
Rice
Slivered almonds
Butter

Sauté the mushrooms in 2 tablespoons of the butter in a skillet until light brown. Spoon into a 3-quart baking dish. Combine the remaining 2 tablespoons butter and the olive oil in the skillet. Add the beef and brown on all sides. Spoon over the mushrooms. Mix 3/4 cup consommé, the wine and soy sauce in a bowl. Pour into the skillet. Dissolve the cornstarch in 1/4 cup consommé. Add to the wine mixture and cook until smooth and thickened, stirring constantly. Fold into the beef and mushrooms. Bake, covered, at 275 degrees for 1 hour. Stir in the soup. Bake for 10 to 15 minutes longer. Season with salt.

Prepare eight servings of rice according to the package directions. Toast slivered almonds in butter in a skillet until golden brown. Fold into the hot cooked rice. Divide the rice among eight dinner plates. Spoon the hot beef mixture over the rice.

SERVES 8

Barbecued Brisket

1 (5- to 6-pound) flat-cut
  beef brisket
3 ounces liquid smoke
Celery salt to taste
Onion salt to taste
Garlic salt to taste

1/4 cup Worcestershire sauce
Salt and pepper to taste
3/4 cup (6 ounces) barbecue sauce
1/2 cup water
2 tablespoons all-purpose flour

Place the brisket flat in an oblong ceramic baking dish. Drizzle with the liquid smoke. Sprinkle with celery salt, onion salt and garlic salt. Chill, covered, for 8 to 10 hours. Drizzle with the Worcestershire sauce. Season with salt and pepper. Cover loosely with foil. Bake at 275 degrees for 5 hours. Remove the foil and pour the barbecue sauce over the brisket. Bake, uncovered, for 1 hour. Remove to a platter and let stand until cool. Slice thinly. Skim the fat from the drippings. Remove the drippings to a saucepan and add the water and flour. Cook until smooth and thickened, stirring constantly. Serve the sauce with the brisket.

SERVES 10

Beef Burgundy

2 (10-ounce) cans beef bouillon or
  beef broth
6 tablespoons all-purpose flour
2 tablespoons tomato paste
2 teaspoons browning sauce
4 pounds beef sirloin or beef
  tenderloin, cut into pieces
1 tablespoon olive oil
1 onion, chopped

1/4 cup sherry
2 cups burgundy
4 (8-ounce) cans
  mushrooms, drained
8 ounces bacon, crisp-cooked
  and crumbled
1 bay leaf
Salt and pepper to taste
Hot cooked pasta or rice

Mix the bouillon, flour, tomato paste and browning sauce in a bowl. Brown the beef in the olive oil in a large heavy saucepan sprayed with nonstick cooking spray; drain as needed. Add the onion and sherry and cook until the onion is translucent. Stir in the bouillon mixture. Add the burgundy, mushrooms, bacon and bay leaf. Season with salt and pepper. Bring to a simmer and simmer for 3 to 4 hours. Remove the bay leaf. Serve over hot cooked pasta or rice.

SERVES 10

"Shoulders which take on responsibilities have no room for chips."

—MARTHA WISE,
NAJA EXECUTIVE
SECRETARY, 1952–1984

Beef Bites

1 (3- to 4-pound) beef chuck roast
1 garlic clove, minced
1/4 cup soy sauce
2 tablespoons water
1 tablespoon vegetable oil
1 tablespoon brown sugar
1/2 teaspoon ginger

Cut the beef into 2- or 3-inch pieces, trimming as much fat as possible. Mix the garlic, soy sauce, water, oil, brown sugar and ginger in a sealable plastic bag. Add the beef and seal tightly. Chill for 3 hours, turning the bag occasionally. Drain, discarding the marinade. Place on a grill over hot coals. Grill to the desired degree of doneness. Serve with hot cooked rice or a baked potato and a green salad.

SERVES 6 TO 8

Sooie Burgers

Ground beef
Pork sausage, casings removed (hot, sage,
    maple and Italian sausage are good
    in this recipe)

Mix equal portions of ground beef and sausage in a bowl. Shape into large patties; the sausage will cause the patties to shrink. Place on a grill over hot coals. Grill until the burgers register 155 degrees or higher on a meat thermometer. Serve with all the burger fixings.

MAKES 3 BURGERS PER 1 POUND OF MEAT

Mississippi Delta Meatballs

Our members gathered at a church to cook for our annual Spaghetti Supper. It was an all-day affair. The sitter hired for our children was late. The kids were banging on the huge pots when, suddenly, two children were missing! Panic reigned! Then a police officer came in, children in tow. He had been delivering his tithe and saw the kids, asleep in the pots!

—JA OF HOPE

MEATBALLS
2 1/4 pounds ground beef
1 cup dry bread crumbs
3/4 cup (4 ounces) grated Romano
   cheese or Parmesan cheese
1/2 cup finely chopped onion
1/4 cup finely chopped celery
1/2 tablespoon parsley flakes, or
   1 tablespoon chopped
   fresh parsley
2 small garlic cloves, minced
Salt and pepper to taste
3 or 4 eggs, lightly beaten

SAUCE
1 small onion, finely chopped
1/2 cup finely chopped celery
1 garlic clove, minced
2 teaspoons parsley flakes, or
   1 tablespoon chopped
   fresh parsley
1/2 cup vegetable oil
8 ounces ground beef
Salt and pepper to taste
2 (15-ounce) cans tomato sauce
10 cups water
7 (6-ounce) cans tomato paste
1 tablespoon sugar
Hot cooked pasta

To prepare the meatballs, mix the ground beef, bread crumbs, cheese, onion, celery, parsley, garlic, salt and pepper in a large bowl. Stir in the eggs. Shape the mixture into twenty-five firm meatballs larger than a golf ball but smaller than a tennis ball. Place slightly separated on lightly oiled rimmed baking sheets. Bake at 350 degrees for 30 to 40 minutes or until cooked through.

To prepare the sauce, cook the onion, celery, garlic and parsley in the oil in a large saucepan until the onion and celery are tender. Add the ground beef. Season with salt and pepper. Cook until the ground beef is brown, stirring until crumbly. Stir in the tomato sauce and 3 to 4 cups of the water. Add the tomato paste and mix well. Stir in the remaining water and the sugar. Bring to a boil, stirring constantly. Reduce the heat to low and simmer for 45 minutes, stirring frequently. Add the meatballs to the sauce and simmer for 1 to 1 1/2 hours. Serve the meatballs and sauce over hot cooked pasta.

To freeze, let the meatballs cool completely after baking. Place in sealable plastic freezer bags. Freeze, laying the bags flat. Let the sauce cool completely. Ladle into 1-gallon sealable plastic bags. Double the bags, if desired. Freeze, laying the bags flat.

MAKES 25 LARGE MEATBALLS

Old-Fashioned Italian Spaghetti

A PLACE CALLED HOPE, *the Junior Auxiliary of Hope, Arkansas cookbook, contains this recipe. The JA of Hope assists the local police department in checking the safety and use of car seats in* CAR SEAT SAFETY.

4 onions, chopped
2 green bell peppers, chopped
1 cup chopped celery
2 garlic cloves, minced
1 tablespoon vegetable oil
3 pounds ground beef
3 (14- or 16-ounce) cans tomatoes
2 (6-ounce) cans tomato paste
2 tablespoons Worcestershire sauce

1 tablespoon salt
2 teaspoons chili powder
1 teaspoon oregano
1/2 teaspoon paprika
1/2 teaspoon pepper
2 bay leaves
Hot red pepper sauce to taste
Beef bouillon as needed
Hot cooked spaghetti

Cook the onions, bell peppers, celery and garlic in the oil in a large saucepan until the onions and celery are translucent. Add the ground beef. Cook until the ground beef is brown, stirring until crumbly; drain. Add the tomatoes, tomato paste, Worcestershire sauce, salt, chili powder, oregano, paprika, pepper, bay leaves and hot sauce. Simmer for 2 hours, stirring frequently. Add the bouillon as needed if the sauce becomes too dry. Remove the bay leaves. Serve over hot cooked spaghetti.

SERVES 14

Johnny Mosette

1¹/2 pounds ground beef
1 green bell pepper, chopped
2 ribs celery, chopped
1 (2-ounce) can mushroom stems
  and pieces
8 ounces onions, chopped
2 garlic cloves, minced
1 (10-ounce) can tomato soup

1 (8-ounce) can tomato sauce
1 (6-ounce) can tomato paste
Salt and pepper to taste
2¹/2 ounces chopped olives
8 ounces mild Cheddar
  cheese, shredded
1 (5- or 6-ounce) package
  egg noodles

Brown the ground beef in a large skillet, stirring until crumbly; drain. Sauté the bell pepper, celery, mushrooms and onions in the skillet or a large saucepan until tender. Stir in the ground beef. Stir in the garlic, soup, tomato sauce and tomato paste. Season with salt and pepper. Bring to a simmer and simmer for 1¹/2 hours, stirring occasionally. Add the olives and cheese to the ground beef mixture and stir until the cheese is melted. Cook the egg noodles according to the package directions; drain. Fold into the ground beef mixture.

SERVES 8

Doritos Delight

The Junior Auxiliary of Winona, Mississippi, is proud of this favorite recipe. A FAMILY IN NEED *project allows the JA of Winona a one-on-one relationship supplying food, clothing, and emotional support for a needy family throughout the year.*

1 pound ground beef
1 (10-ounce) can cream of
  mushroom soup
1 (10-ounce) can cream of
  chicken soup
1 (12-ounce) can evaporated milk

1 (4-ounce) can chopped
  green chiles
1 (12-ounce) package
  Doritos, crushed
Shredded Cheddar cheese

Brown the ground beef in a skillet, stirring until crumbly; drain. Mix the mushroom soup, chicken soup and evaporated milk in a large saucepan and heat through. Stir in the ground beef and green chiles. Spread the Doritos over the bottom of a 9×13-inch baking dish. Layer the ground beef and cheese over the top. Bake at 350 degrees for 20 minutes.

SERVES 6

Hodge Podge and Cheese Boxes

HODGE PODGE
1 1/2 pounds ground beef
1 1/2 cups chopped celery
1 1/2 cups chopped onions
2 (15-ounce) cans ranch-style beans
3 (10-ounce) cans minestrone
1 cup water
1 (10-ounce) can chopped
  tomatoes with green chiles
2 tablespoons (scant) chili powder

2 teaspoons Worcestershire sauce
Garlic salt to taste

CHEESE BOXES
2 (5-ounce) jars sharp Old English
  cheese spread
1/2 cup (1 stick) margarine, melted
1 egg, lightly beaten
1 loaf sandwich bread,
  crusts trimmed

To prepare the hodge podge, brown the ground beef with the celery and onions in a large heavy saucepan, stirring until the ground beef is crumbly; drain. Stir in the beans, soup, water, tomatoes with green chiles, chili powder and Worcestershire sauce. Season with the garlic salt. Bring to a simmer and simmer for 25 minutes.

To prepare the cheese boxes, beat the cheese spread, margarine and egg in a mixing bowl until smooth. Make sandwiches by layering three slices of bread, spreading the bottom two slices with the cheese mixture. Repeat with the remaining ingredients. Cut each sandwich into thirds and place on a baking sheet. Bake at 350 degrees for 20 minutes.

Serve the hodge podge spooned over the cheese boxes or serve the cheese boxes on the side.

SERVES 6 TO 8

Veal Scaloppini with Lemon Sauce

The Junior Auxiliary of Houma, Louisiana, includes this recipe in their cookbook, Bayou Breezes. *The JA of Houma provides emergency relief for families with the* Hearts to Hands *project.*

1¹/2 pounds veal cutlets
¹/3 cup all-purpose flour
¹/2 teaspoon salt
¹/4 teaspoon pepper
1 tablespoon olive oil
3 tablespoons butter

¹/2 cup dry white wine
3 tablespoons lemon juice
1 large garlic clove, pressed
2 tablespoons capers
2 tablespoons chopped
    fresh parsley

Pound the veal between sheets of heavy-duty plastic wrap with a mallet or rolling pin until flattened to ¹/4 inch thick. Mix the flour, salt and pepper in a shallow dish. Dredge the veal in the flour mixture, shaking off any excess. Cook the veal in batches in the olive oil and 2 tablespoons of the butter in a large skillet over medium-high heat for 2 minutes or until golden brown and cooked through, turning once. Remove the veal from the skillet and keep warm, reserving the pan drippings.

Add the remaining 1 tablespoon butter, the wine and lemon juice to the drippings in the skillet. Cook until heated through, stirring constantly and scraping up any brown bits from the bottom of the skillet. Stir in the garlic, capers and parsley. Spoon over the veal and serve immediately. Serve with hot cooked angel hair pasta, if desired.

For a variation, substitute 4 boneless skinless chicken breasts for the veal. Extend the cooking time to 6 minutes or until golden brown and cooked through, turning once.

Serves 4 to 6

I was frustrated by the lack of progress I was making with the child I was tutoring each week in the public housing project. "Twelve divided by four is three," he said as he rolled his eyes. Then, in a small voice he added, "Even your mouth smells good." I had forgotten that even toothpaste can be a luxury and what I was teaching was not all in books.

—Project Backpack

Veal Piccata Pasta

1 pound veal cutlets (6 to 8),
    pounded 1/8 to 1/4 inch thick
Salt and pepper to taste
1 cup all-purpose flour
1 tablespoon Creole seasoning
1 tablespoon Greek seasoning
1/4 cup olive oil

1 tablespoon butter
3/4 cup dry white wine
1 tablespoon butter
1/4 cup lemon juice
1/2 (3-ounce) jar capers, drained
1 (12-ounce) package angel
    hair pasta

Season the veal lightly with salt and pepper. Mix the flour, Creole seasoning and
Greek seasoning in a shallow dish. Dredge the veal in the flour mixture, shaking
off any excess. Cook in two batches in the olive oil and 1 tablespoon butter in a
large skillet over medium heat for 40 seconds or until golden brown and cooked
through, turning once. Remove the veal and set aside. Increase the heat to high.
Add the wine to the drippings in the skillet. Cook until reduced slightly, stirring
constantly and scraping any brown bits from the bottom of the skillet. Stir in
1 tablespoon butter, the lemon juice and capers. Reduce the heat to medium
and return the veal to the skillet. Cook for 1 minute or until heated through,
constantly turning the veal and coating with the sauce.

Cook the pasta according to the package directions; drain. Serve the veal and
sauce over the pasta. Asparagus pairs well with this dish.

Serves 3 to 4

Bourbon-Marinated Pork Tenderloin

4 garlic cloves, minced
3/4 cup soy sauce
1/2 cup bourbon
1/4 cup Worcestershire sauce
1/4 cup olive oil

1/4 cup water
3 tablespoons dark brown sugar
1/2 teaspoon ginger
2 tablespoons pepper
2 1/2 pounds pork tenderloin (1 to 2)

Mix the garlic, soy sauce, bourbon, Worcestershire sauce, olive oil, water, brown
sugar, ginger and pepper in a sealable plastic bag or shallow baking dish. Add the
pork and turn until coated. Chill, tightly sealed or covered, for 4 to 24 hours.
Drain, reserving the marinade. Place on a grill over medium-hot coals. Grill until
a meat thermometer inserted into the thickest part of the tenderloin registers
160 degrees, turning once. Bring the reserved marinade to a boil in a saucepan and
boil for 1 minute. Serve the sauce on the side. Garnish with sprigs of fresh parsley.

Serves 4 to 6

Pork Tenderloin with Comeback Sauce

"Lunch Buddies is a project for children whom school counselors felt would benefit from a relationship with a mentor. I was paired with a first-grade girl with an unstable home life. Our relationship was so good that it continued throughout my years in JA. She is now in the ninth grade, but I still have lunch with her once a month. Most junior high students would be embarrassed, but she is still delighted when I come. I plan to be at her college graduation."

—LIFE MEMBER,
JA OF JONESBORO

COMEBACK SAUCE
1 onion, minced
2 garlic cloves, minced
1 cup mayonnaise
1/2 cup olive oil
1/3 cup chili sauce
1/4 cup ketchup
2 tablespoons water
4 teaspoons Worcestershire sauce
4 teaspoons mustard
2 teaspoons coarsely ground pepper
1/4 teaspoon hot red pepper sauce
1/8 teaspoon paprika

PORK TENDERLOIN
1/2 cup olive oil
8 fresh thyme sprigs
2 green onions, chopped
2 tablespoons horseradish
2 teaspoons salt
2 teaspoons pepper
1 (2-pound) pork tenderloin

To prepare the sauce, whisk the onion, garlic, mayonnaise, olive oil, chili sauce, ketchup, water, Worcestershire sauce, mustard, pepper, hot sauce and paprika in a bowl until blended. Chill, covered, until serving time.

To prepare the pork tenderloin, mix the olive oil, thyme, green onions, horseradish, salt and pepper in a sealable plastic bag. Add the pork and turn until coated. Seal tightly and chill for 8 to 10 hours, turning occasionally. Drain, discarding the marinade. Place the pork on a rimmed baking sheet. Broil 6 inches from the heat source for 5 minutes. Bake at 425 degrees for 20 minutes or until cooked through. Serve with the sauce.

SERVES 4 TO 6

Grilled Garlic and Herb Pork Tenderloin

1/2 cup extra-virgin olive oil
1/4 cup red wine vinegar
6 garlic cloves, minced

1/2 teaspoon dried thyme, dried oregano or dried rosemary
1 (2- to 2 1/2-pound) pork tenderloin

Whisk the olive oil, vinegar, garlic and thyme in a bowl until blended. Combine the pork and marinade in a sealable plastic bag, turning the pork until coated. Seal tightly and chill for 4 hours, turning occasionally. Drain, discarding the marinade. Place on a grill over hot coals. Grill until cooked through. Serve warm or cold. The pork may be frozen in its marinade. Allow to thaw completely in the refrigerator before grilling.

SERVES 6 TO 8

Tuscan Pork Chops

RENDEZVOUS ON THE RIDGE *includes this recipe from the Junior Auxiliary of Jonesboro, Arkansas. The JA of Jonesboro members serve as role models for at-risk students in the* LUNCH BUDDIES *project.*

1/4 cup all-purpose flour
1 teaspoon salt
3/4 teaspoon seasoned pepper
4 (1-inch-thick) boneless pork chops
1 tablespoon olive oil

3 or 4 garlic cloves, minced
1/3 cup balsamic vinegar
1/3 cup chicken broth
3 plum tomatoes, seeded and chopped
2 tablespoons capers

Mix the flour, salt and pepper in a shallow baking dish. Dredge the pork chops in the flour mixture, shaking off any excess. Cook in the hot olive oil in a large nonstick skillet for 2 to 4 minutes or until golden brown, turning once. Remove the pork chops from the skillet. Sauté the garlic in the drippings in the skillet for 1 minute. Add the vinegar and broth. Cook until heated through, stirring constantly and scraping up any brown bits from the bottom of the skillet. Stir in the tomatoes and capers. Return the pork chops to the skillet and bring the liquid to a boil. Reduce the heat and simmer, covered, for 4 to 5 minutes or until the pork is cooked through. Serve with hot cooked pasta tossed with a garlic butter sauce, if desired, and garnish with sprigs of fresh parsley.

SERVES 4

AWARD WINNER:

MAKING THE

CONNECTION—JA OF

MADISON COUNTY

This was an education

project for the JA chapter

members that focused on

improving communication

skills used when connecting

with those of a different

socioeconomic background.

The objective was to seek

advice and information

on how to create genuine

connections with those

whom we serve, being

sensitive to the fact that

many recipients have a

home life that is far

different than that of a

JA member.

Asian Sesame Baby Back Ribs

This recipe is a favorite of the Junior Auxiliary of Madison County, Florida. The JA of Madison County teaches self-esteem to young children with the SOOPER PUPPY *program.*

2 tablespoons paprika	1 (12-ounce) jar orange marmalade
1¹/₂ teaspoons cayenne pepper	6 tablespoons balsamic vinegar
1 tablespoon salt	¹/₄ cup plus 1 tablespoon packed
1 tablespoon black pepper	light brown sugar
2 racks baby back pork ribs	6 dashes of soy sauce
3 tablespoons vegetable oil	2 tablespoons sesame seeds

Combine the paprika, cayenne pepper, salt and black pepper in a small bowl and mix well. Brush both sides of the ribs with the oil. Season both sides with the spice mixture. Place bone side up on one large or two small foil-lined rimmed baking sheets. Bake at 350 degrees for 1 hour. Turn and bake for 45 minutes. Process the marmalade, vinegar, brown sugar and soy sauce in a food processor until smooth. Brush one-fourth of the marmalade mixture on each side of the ribs. Bake for 15 minutes longer. Remove the ribs to a platter and let stand until cool. Cut into individual ribs. Brush each with the remaining marmalade mixture. Return the ribs to the baking sheet and sprinkle with the sesame seeds. Bake for 10 minutes.

SERVES 6

Venison Steak

2 venison steaks, cut into	1 cup mustard
bite-size pieces	2 to 4 cups water
Salt and pepper to taste	Hot cooked rice
1 onion, chopped	

Season the venison with salt and pepper. Combine the venison and onion in a large cast-iron skillet. Add the mustard and toss until coated. Cook over medium heat until very charred on the outside. Stir in the water. Reduce the heat to low and cook, covered, for 1 hour. Serve over rice. For a variation, substitute beef round steak for the venison.

SERVES 2

Award-Winning Venison Chili

The Junior Auxiliary of Collierville, Tennessee, submitted this recipe from the chapter's cookbook, Classically Collierville: Food For Family and Friends. *The JA of Collierville hosts holiday events for clients at the Page Robbins Adult Day Care Center.*

2 pounds ground venison
1 onion, chopped
2 garlic cloves, minced
2 (15-ounce) cans crushed tomatoes
1 (15-ounce) can kidney beans
2 cups tomato and basil pasta sauce

2 tablespoons red wine vinegar
1 teaspoon cumin
1 teaspoon basil
1 teaspoon oregano
6 to 8 tablespoons chili powder
Salt and pepper to taste

Brown the venison with the onion and garlic in a large saucepan, stirring until the venison is crumbly; drain. Stir in the tomatoes, beans, pasta sauce, vinegar, cumin, basil, oregano and chili powder. Season with salt and pepper. Bring to a boil. Reduce the heat and simmer for 20 minutes or longer. This dish gets better the longer it simmers and the longer it sits to allow the flavors to blend.

Serves 8 to 10

Grilled Duck Breasts

1 cup red wine vinegar
1 cup olive oil
1/4 cup Worcestershire sauce
1 teaspoon salt
1 teaspoon meat tenderizer
1/2 teaspoon tarragon

1/2 teaspoon pepper
1/4 teaspoon garlic
2 bay leaves
2 to 4 wild duck breasts
Bacon slices

Whisk the vinegar, olive oil, Worcestershire sauce, salt, meat tenderizer, tarragon, pepper, garlic and bay leaves in a bowl until mixed well. Add the duck and turn until coated. Chill, covered, for 24 hours. Drain, reserving the marinade. Wrap the duck with bacon and secure with wooden picks. Place on a grill over medium-hot coals. Grill until cooked through, turning and basting frequently with the reserved marinade. Discard the bay leaves.

Serves 2 to 4

Chicken & Seafood

"I'll Never Be in JA!"

THOSE WERE THE WORDS I REPEATED WHEN MY MOTHER, EVA JOHNSON, A JUNIOR AUXILIARY MEMBER FROM THE NASHVILLE, AR, CHAPTER, WOULD ROUSE ME FROM MY SATURDAY MORNING SLEEP TO ACCOMPANY HER TO WORK IN HER SERVICE PROJECT, THE "JA THRIFT SHOP." I GRIPED ABOUT GETTING OUT OF BED AND HAVING TO SIT IN THAT BORING STORE AND HELP SORT DONATED CLOTHES FOR THE LESS FORTUNATE.

I fussed when she made me work on PR by making signs and riding in parades promoting the JA's upcoming "Follies" to raise money. I certainly couldn't understand why I had to stand up with a ukulele and humiliate myself by singing in it! I really rolled my eyes when she made me go with her on all those Christmas Eves to deliver food baskets and toys to needy families. I had to wait on her forever while she visited with these people and gave them money to pay their electric bills. I watched her hold babies in urine-soaked diapers, and then I endured the stench when she got it on her clothes and we got back in our warm car to go to our cozy home with all our presents. ➤

But I did notice the people who came to get the clothing in that store and had the food and presents delivered so Santa could be everywhere. I saw the desperation in their eyes and the gratitude on their dirty, tear-stained faces. As I grew up, I kept watching my mother.

And when someone asked me to be a JA member years later, I had changed my mind.

Let your children see you make a difference. Let them watch you as you change lives. You never know when you are modeling volunteerism for someone who may grow up to be a NAJA President or for someone even more special . . . just like you!

Thanks, Mom.

Suzanna Johnson Clark
NAJA President 2002–03

Rosemary Chicken Pizza

The Junior Auxiliary of Jackson County, Arkansas, submitted the following recipe. The JA of Jackson County's project, House of Mary, *supplies materials for a battered women's shelter.*

2 boneless chicken breasts,
   cut into strips
1 onion, sliced
1/2 teaspoon crushed rosemary
1 tablespoon olive oil
1 uncooked (12-inch) pizza crust

1 (14-ounce) can chunky
   tomatoes, drained
2 cups (8 ounces) shredded
   mozzarella cheese
1 green, yellow or red bell
   pepper, chopped

Sauté the chicken, onion and rosemary in the olive oil in a skillet until the chicken is cooked through; drain. Place the crust on a baking sheet. Layer the tomatoes, half the cheese, the chicken mixture, bell pepper and remaining cheese over the crust. Bake at 450 degrees for 10 minutes or until bubbly and heated through.

Serves 4 to 6

Cranberry Chicken

1/2 cup all-purpose flour
1/2 teaspoon salt
1/4 teaspoon pepper
6 (4-ounce) boneless skinless
   chicken breasts
3 tablespoons margarine
1 cup fresh or frozen cranberries

1 cup water
1/2 cup packed brown sugar
1 dash of nutmeg
1 tablespoon red wine vinegar or
   apple cider vinegar (optional)
Hot cooked rice (optional)

Mix the flour, salt and pepper in a shallow dish. Dredge the chicken in the flour mixture, shaking off any excess. Brown both sides of the chicken in the margarine in a skillet. Remove from the skillet and keep warm. Cook the cranberries, water, brown sugar, nutmeg and vinegar in the drippings in the skillet for 5 minutes or until the cranberries burst, stirring constantly. Add the chicken and simmer, covered, for 20 to 30 minutes or until the chicken is cooked through and tender, basting occasionally with the sauce. Serve over hot cooked rice, if desired.

Serves 6

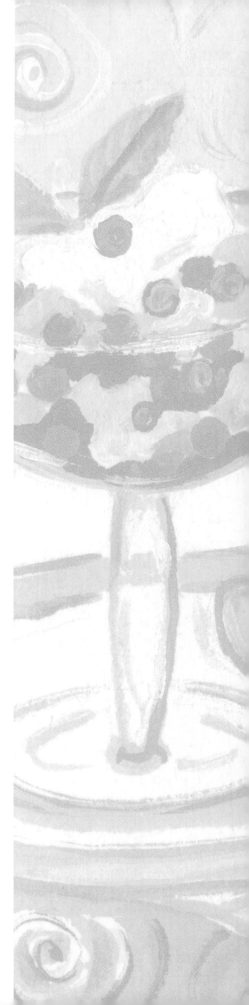

Braised Barbecued Chicken

AWARD WINNER:
REMEMBER YOUR ABCs—
JA OF BROOKHAVEN

Nationwide, only about 6 percent of older children are properly restrained in a booster seat, even though car crashes are one of the leading causes of death. Focusing on children ages four through eight, our chapter implemented a multi-pronged approach to educate parents, teachers, and the children themselves on the importance of using a lifesaving booster seat. All events were in conjunction with National Car Safety Week, February 9–13, 2004.

1/2 cup orange juice
1/2 cup pineapple juice
1 tablespoon cornstarch
2 garlic cloves, minced
1/3 cup soy sauce
1/3 cup packed brown sugar
3 tablespoons ketchup
3 tablespoons apple cider vinegar
2 tablespoons ginger
1/2 teaspoon crushed red pepper flakes
4 chicken breasts
2 tablespoons vegetable oil
2 cups hot cooked rice
1/4 cup chopped green onions

Mix the orange juice and pineapple juice in a bowl. Mix 1 tablespoon of the orange juice mixture and the cornstarch in a small bowl until smooth; set aside. Stir the garlic, soy sauce, brown sugar, ketchup, vinegar, ginger and red pepper flakes into the remaining orange juice mixture.

Cook the chicken in the oil in a skillet for 6 minutes or until golden brown, turning once. Pour the soy sauce mixture over the chicken and bring the liquid to a boil. Reduce the heat and simmer, covered, for 35 minutes. Stir in the cornstarch mixture. Cook for 5 minutes longer, stirring constantly.

Serve the chicken with the rice. Top with the green onions.

SERVES 4

Bourbon Chicken

The Junior Auxiliary of Kosciusko, Mississippi, contributed this recipe. The JA of Kosciusko teaches traffic and bicycle safety to school children with the SAFETY TOWN *project.*

4 boneless skinless chicken breasts, chopped
3/4 cup packed brown sugar
1/2 cup soy sauce
1/4 cup bourbon
2 tablespoons dried minced onion
1 teaspoon ginger
1/2 teaspoon garlic powder

Place the chicken in a 9×13-inch baking dish. Mix the brown sugar, soy sauce, bourbon, onion, ginger and garlic powder in a bowl. Pour over the chicken. Chill, covered, for 8 to 10 hours. Bake at 325 degrees for 1 hour or until the chicken is brown and cooked through, basting frequently with the sauce.

SERVES 4

Chicken Piccata

The Junior League of Brookhaven, Mississippi, donated the following recipe. The JA of Brookhaven won the Norma DeLong Education Award in 2004 for REMEMBER YOUR ABCs.

2 chicken breasts, cut into halves
Salt and pepper to taste
All-purpose flour
2 tablespoons olive oil
1/4 cup white wine
1 teaspoon minced garlic
1/2 cup chicken broth
2 tablespoons fresh lemon juice
1 tablespoon drained capers
2 tablespoons butter
Fresh lemon slices
Hot cooked angel hair pasta

Flatten the chicken with a mallet. Season with salt and pepper and dust with flour. Cook the chicken in the olive oil in a skillet for 4 minutes, turning once. Remove the chicken from the skillet and keep warm, reserving the drippings in the skillet. Add the wine and garlic to the reserved drippings in the skillet. Cook for 2 minutes or until the garlic is light brown and the skillet is almost dry, stirring constantly and scraping up any brown bits from the bottom of the skillet. Add the broth, lemon juice and capers. Add the chicken and cook for 2 minutes or until the chicken is cooked through, turning once. Divide the hot cooked pasta among dinner plates and top with the chicken. Add the butter and lemon slices to the sauce. Stir constantly until the butter is melted. Spoon over the chicken and pasta. Garnish with chopped fresh parsley.

SERVES 2 TO 4

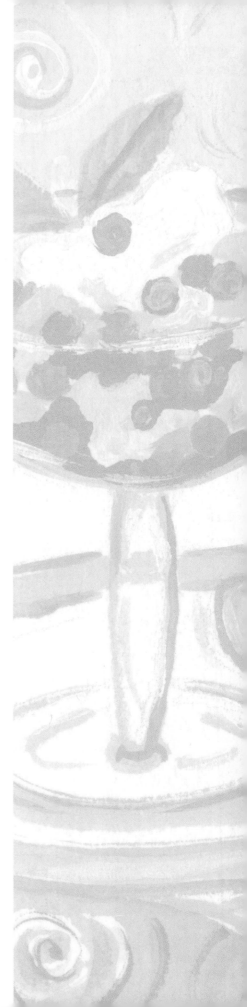

Dijon Chicken and Mushrooms

AWARD WINNER:

SUNSHINE SCHOOL—

JA OF SEARCY

The Sunshine School in Searcy, Arkansas, was founded in 1965 after several Junior Auxiliary members attended a meeting of the White County Association of Retarded Citizens. Parents desperately needed day care for their physically and mentally challenged children. JA members helped with both funding and volunteering their assistance. In the beginning, there were eight students who attended two days a week. Today, there are twenty staff members who accommodate sixty students attending five days a week.

This is a favorite recipe of the Junior Auxiliary of Searcy, Arkansas. The JA of Searcy provides meals and immunizations for children through the SHOTS FOR TOTS *project.*

4 (6-ounce) boneless skinless chicken breasts
Salt and pepper to taste
2 tablespoons butter
8 white button mushrooms, finely chopped
1 (10-ounce) can fat-free condensed cream of mushroom soup

1/2 cup chicken broth
1/4 cup Dijon mustard
2 tablespoons deli-style brown mustard
1 tomato, chopped
1/4 cup frozen corn kernels, thawed
1/4 cup chopped fresh chives

Season the chicken with salt and pepper. Cook in the butter in a skillet over medium-high heat for 8 minutes or until brown, turning once. Remove the chicken to a platter, reserving the drippings in the skillet. Cook the mushrooms in the reserved drippings in the skillet for 3 minutes or until tender. Whisk in the soup, broth, Dijon mustard and brown mustard. Bring to a simmer and add the chicken, submerging the chicken in the liquid. Reduce the heat to medium-low. Cook, covered, for 10 minutes or until the sauce is thickened and the chicken is cooked through. Remove from the heat and sprinkle with the tomato, corn and chives. Serve hot.

SERVES 4

Grilled Basil Chicken

1/2 cup (1 stick) butter, softened
2 tablespoons minced fresh basil
1 tablespoon grated Parmesan
   cheese
1/4 teaspoon garlic powder
1/8 teaspoon salt

1/8 teaspoon pepper
4 boneless skinless chicken breasts
3/4 teaspoon coarsely ground
   pepper
1/3 cup margarine, melted
2 tablespoons minced fresh basil

Combine the butter, 2 tablespoons basil, the cheese, garlic powder, salt and 1/8 teaspoon pepper in a mixing bowl. Beat until light and fluffy. Spoon into a small bowl and set aside.

Season the chicken with 3/4 teaspoon pepper. Mix the margarine and 2 tablespoons basil in a bowl. Brush over the chicken. Place on a grill over medium-hot coals. Grill for 16 to 20 minutes or until cooked through, turning once and basting frequently with the margarine mixture. Serve the chicken with the basil butter.

Serves 4

Basil Chicken Strips

SOUTHERN GENERATIONS, *the cookbook from the Junior Auxiliary of Starkville, Mississippi, includes this recipe. The JA of Starkville fingerprints area kindergarten students for family records with the* KINDER PRINT *project.*

8 ounces chicken tenderloin pieces
2 tablespoons all-purpose flour
1 teaspoon garlic salt

3 tablespoons butter or margarine
2 tablespoons red wine vinegar
1/2 teaspoon dried basil

Combine the chicken, flour and garlic salt in a sealable plastic bag. Seal tightly and shake until the chicken is coated. Cook the chicken in the butter in a skillet over medium-high heat for 5 minutes. Stir in the vinegar and basil and cook until the chicken is cooked through.

Serves 3 to 4

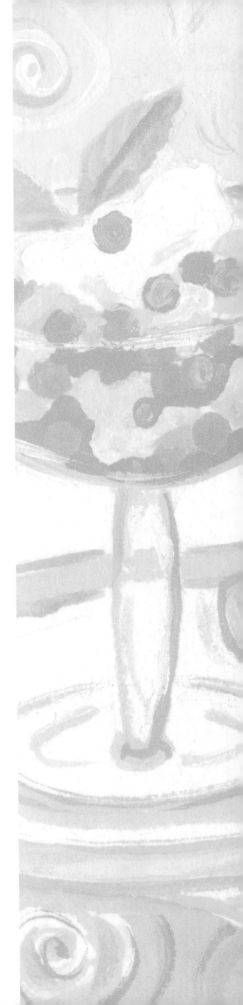

JA Crown Clubs

You can never be too young to learn about commitment and service. JA chapters determined that training volunteers early produced a lifestyle of caring for others. Many chapters have adopted projects to establish CROWN CLUBS made up of high school students willing to learn to give to others in need. The fine tradition of community service begun in 1941 expands and continues with each new generation trained by JA.

Chicken Little Fingers with Plum Sauce

Chicken Little Fingers
6 whole boneless chicken breasts
2 garlic cloves, minced
1 1/2 cups buttermilk
1 tablespoon lemon juice
2 teaspoons Worcestershire sauce
1 teaspoon soy sauce
1 teaspoon paprika
1 teaspoon salt
1 teaspoon pepper

4 cups bread crumbs
1/2 cup sesame seeds
1/2 cup (1 stick) butter
1/2 cup shortening

Plum Sauce
1 1/2 cups red plum jelly
1 1/2 tablespoons mustard
1 1/2 tablespoons horseradish
1 1/2 tablespoons lemon juice

To prepare the chicken, cut the chicken into 1/2-inch-thick strips. Mix the garlic, buttermilk, lemon juice, Worcestershire sauce, soy sauce, paprika, salt and pepper in a bowl. Add the chicken and toss until coated. Chill, covered, for 8 to 10 hours. Drain, discarding the marinade.

Mix the bread crumbs and sesame seeds in a large bowl. Add the chicken and toss until coated. Arrange in a greased baking dish or baking sheet. Melt the butter and shortening together in a saucepan and stir until blended. Brush over the chicken. Bake at 350 degrees for 35 to 40 minutes or until cooked through.

To prepare the sauce, mix the jelly, mustard, horseradish and lemon juice in a saucepan. Cook over low heat until heated through, stirring constantly. Serve with the chicken.

Serves 6 to 8

Chicken and Dumplings

1 onion, quartered	1 tablespoon shortening
1 rib celery, quartered	2 cups all-purpose flour
6 cups water	1/2 cup cold water
1 teaspoon salt	1 dash of salt
1/2 teaspoon pepper	1/4 cup milk
1 (3- to 4-pound) chicken	1 tablespoon butter

Stuff the onion and celery into the cavity of the chicken. Bring 6 cups water, 1 teaspoon salt and the pepper to a boil in a saucepan. Add the chicken and cook until cooked through. Drain, reserving the broth. Maintain the temperature of the broth. Debone the chicken.

Cut the shortening into the flour in a bowl until crumbly. Add 1/2 cup cold water and a dash of salt. Stir until combined. Roll the dough out thinly and cut into squares. Bring the reserved broth to a boil. Drop in the dumplings one at a time. Reduce the heat to medium-low. Cook, covered, for 10 to 12 minutes. Add the chicken. Stir in the milk and butter. Cook until heated through.

SERVES 6

Chicken Sauterne

6 boneless chicken breasts	1 1/2 cups sauterne
2 envelopes spaghetti sauce mix	1 (8-ounce) can
1/4 cup (1/2 stick) butter	mushrooms, drained

Toss the chicken with 1 envelope of the spaghetti sauce mix in a bowl until coated. Cook the chicken in the butter in a skillet until brown on both sides. Remove to a baking dish and drizzle with the wine. Arrange the mushrooms on top. Sprinkle with the remaining envelope of spaghetti sauce mix. Bake at 325 degrees for 40 minutes or until the chicken is cooked through.

SERVES 6

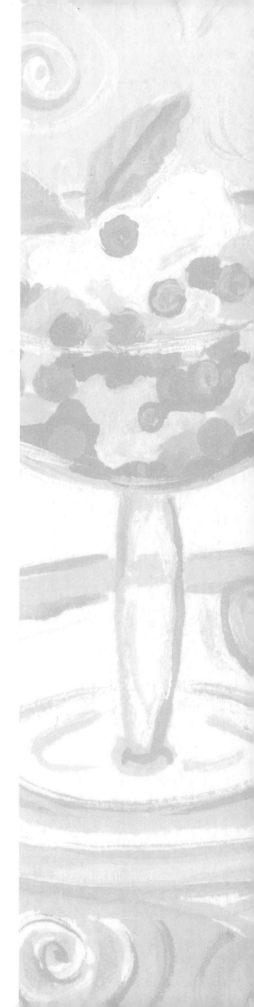

Chicken, Mushroom and Artichoke Bake

4 to 6 boneless chicken breasts
Salt and pepper to taste
Paprika to taste
1/2 cup (1 stick) butter
8 to 16 ounces mushrooms, sliced

2 tablespoons all-purpose flour
1 (10-ounce) can chicken broth
1/2 cup sherry or other wine
1 (14-ounce) can artichoke
  hearts, drained

Season the chicken with salt, pepper and paprika. Cook in the butter in a skillet until light brown on both sides. Remove the chicken to a baking dish, reserving the drippings in the skillet. Sauté the mushrooms in the reserved drippings in the skillet until tender. Stir in the flour. Stir in the broth and sherry. Season with salt and pepper. Simmer for 5 to 10 minutes, stirring frequently. Pour over the chicken. Bake at 375 degrees for 1 hour. Top with the artichoke hearts and bake for 20 minutes longer.

SERVES 4 TO 6

Poulet de Normande

The Junior Auxiliary of Lawrence County, Tennessee, donated this favorite recipe. The JA of Lawrence County hosts a job interview training session for unemployed women with the DRESS FOR SUCCESS *project.*

3 cups chopped cooked chicken
1 (8-ounce) package herb-seasoned
  stuffing mix
1 bunch green onions, chopped
1/2 cup chopped celery
1 1/2 cups milk
1 cup chicken broth
1/2 cup mayonnaise

1/2 cup (1 stick) butter or
  margarine, melted
2 eggs, lightly beaten
1/2 teaspoon salt
1 (10-ounce) can cream of
  mushroom soup
1 cup (4 ounces) shredded
  Cheddar cheese

Mix the chicken, stuffing mix, green onions and celery in a large bowl. Stir in the milk, broth, mayonnaise, butter, eggs and salt. Spoon into a 9×13-inch glass baking dish sprayed with nonstick cooking spray. Spread the soup over the top and sprinkle with the cheese. Chill, covered, for 8 to 10 hours. Bake at 325 degrees for 45 minutes. Let stand for 3 to 4 minutes before serving. This dish freezes well once assembled.

SERVES 12

Swiss Chicken Bake

4 bone-in chicken breasts,
  skin removed
Salt and pepper to taste
8 slices Swiss cheese
1 (10-ounce) can cream of
  chicken soup
1/2 cup mushrooms
1/2 cup white wine
1 1/2 cups stuffing mix
3 tablespoons butter, melted

Place the chicken bone side down in a baking dish. Season with salt and pepper. Top each piece of chicken with two slices of cheese. Mix the soup, mushrooms and wine in a bowl. Pour over the cheese. Sprinkle with the stuffing mix and drizzle with the butter. Bake at 350 degrees for 1 hour.

SERVES 4

Hot Chicken Salad

The Junior Auxiliary of Madison-Ridgeland, Mississippi, submitted this recipe. The JA of Madison-Ridgeland mentors children in a community children's home through the SUNNYBROOK project.

1 cup mayonnaise
3/4 cup (3 ounces) shredded
  Cheddar cheese
1/2 (10-ounce) can cream of
  chicken soup
1 tablespoon lemon juice
1 teaspoon garlic salt
2 cups chopped cooked chicken
2 ribs celery, chopped
1 small red onion, chopped, or
  1 bunch green onions, chopped
1 (8-ounce) can water chestnuts,
  drained and chopped (optional)
1/2 cup toasted almonds

Mix the mayonnaise, cheese, soup, lemon juice and garlic salt in a bowl. Stir in the chicken, celery, onion, water chestnuts and almonds. Spoon into a baking dish. Bake at 375 degrees for 15 minutes or until the chicken salad is heated through and the cheese is melted.

SERVES 6

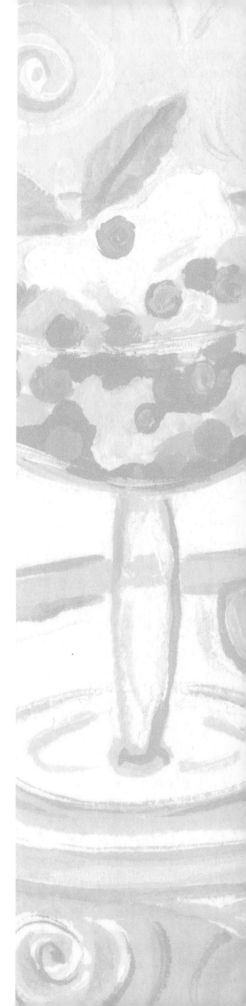

JUNIOR AUXILIARY-ITIS

"The spirit of Junior Auxiliary is a disease . . . for victims of severe cases there is no known cure. It is our goal to infect as many women in as many states as possible . . . Contrary to most infections, strength, rather than weakness, results from epidemics . . . Certain mannerisms become noticeable: a warm heart, kindly feelings, tolerance, patience, and clear sparkling eyes . . . This is the one disease that we hope will flourish."

—SIDDY AGNEW, REGION 1 DIRECTOR, 1961

Sunday Chicken and Seafood Casserole

1 pound crab meat
6 boneless chicken breast fillets
Water
Salt and pepper to taste
1/4 cup (1/2 stick) butter
3/4 cup all-purpose flour
3 cups hot milk
1 tablespoon Worcestershire sauce
1/2 cup sherry
16 ounces mushrooms, sliced

Butter for sautéing
2 (14-ounce) cans artichoke
   hearts, drained
1 pound boiled shrimp, peeled
1/2 cup (2 ounces) grated
   Parmesan cheese
2 tablespoons chopped
   fresh parsley
Paprika to taste

Wash and drain the crab meat. Pick through the crab meat gently, discarding any bits of shell or cartilage; set aside. Cook the chicken in water seasoned with salt and pepper in a large saucepan until cooked through. Drain, discarding the liquid. Remove the skin and chop the chicken. Melt 1/4 cup butter in a saucepan. Add the flour gradually, stirring constantly until blended. Add the milk gradually, stirring constantly until blended. Stir in the Worcestershire sauce and sherry. Season with salt and pepper. Sauté the mushrooms in butter in a skillet until tender; drain. Layer the artichoke hearts, chicken, shrimp, crab meat, mushrooms and sherry sauce in a 9×13-inch buttered baking dish. Sprinkle with the cheese, parsley and paprika. Bake at 375 degrees for 40 minutes.

SERVES 12

Crab and Shrimp Casserole

1 green bell pepper, chopped
1 onion, chopped
1/2 cup chopped celery
1 1/4 cups mayonnaise
2 teaspoons Worcestershire sauce

1 pound cooked peeled shrimp
1 pound lump crab meat
Salt and pepper to taste
1 cup bread crumbs

Mix the bell pepper, onion, celery, mayonnaise and Worcestershire sauce in a bowl. Fold in the shrimp and crab meat. Season with salt and pepper. Spoon into a 3-quart glass baking dish. Sprinkle with the bread crumbs. Bake at 350 degrees for 1 hour or until bubbly. This recipe may be doubled or tripled.

SERVES 4 TO 6

Fireman Grilled Shrimp

The Junior Auxiliary of Hammond, Louisiana, submitted this recipe. The JA of Hammond decorates children's rooms in HABITAT FOR HUMANITY *homes in the community.*

5 pounds Gulf shrimp,
   heads removed
1 1/2 cups (3 sticks) butter
1/2 cup (1 stick) margarine
1 (12-ounce) bottle beer
Juice of 3 lemons
1 tablespoon Creole seasoning

1 tablespoon crab boil
1 tablespoon rosemary
1 tablespoon thyme
2 bay leaves
Hot cooked angel hair pasta
   (optional)

Arrange the shrimp closely in a single layer in a large baking dish. Melt the butter and margarine in a saucepan. Stir in the beer, lemon juice, Creole seasoning, crab boil, rosemary, thyme and bay leaves. Pour over the shrimp. Add additional beer and butter if needed to cover the shrimp. Bake at 350 degrees for 15 to 20 minutes or until the shells begin to loosen from the shrimp. Discard the bay leaves. Spoon over hot cooked angel hair pasta or serve with crusty bread to dip in the sauce.

SERVES 12

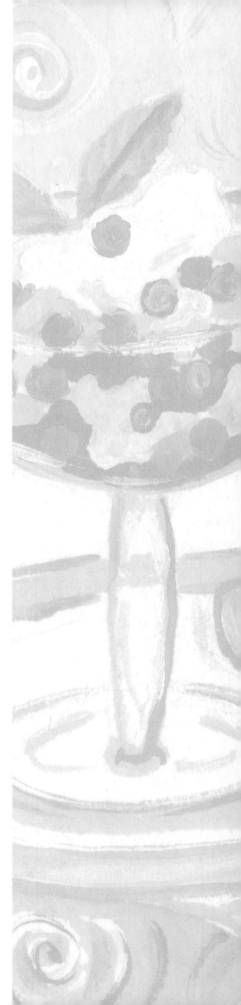

Shrimp and Grits

RED RIBBON WEEK

JA of Jonesboro champions a drug-free environment for its students. One week each year, everyone wears red ribbons that read, "I've got better things to do than drugs!" To kick off the week, students release a red balloon containing handwritten notes encouraging the finder to live a drug-free life. In 2005, an Amish boy from Pennsylvania found the balloon and became pen pals with the Jonesboro note-writer, enabling classmates to learn about the traditions of the Amish and life in Pennsylvania. It was a blessing to everyone involved!

2 cups water
1 (14-ounce) can chicken broth
3/4 cup half-and-half
3/4 teaspoon salt
1 cup grits
3/4 cup (3 ounces) shredded
   Cheddar cheese
1/4 cup (1 ounce) shredded
   Parmesan cheese
2 tablespoons butter
1/2 teaspoon hot red pepper sauce
1/4 teaspoon white pepper

3 slices bacon
1 pound shrimp, peeled
   and deveined
1/8 teaspoon salt
1/4 teaspoon black pepper
1/4 cup all-purpose flour
1 cup sliced mushrooms
1/2 cup chopped green onions
2 garlic cloves, minced
1/2 cup low-sodium chicken broth
2 tablespoons fresh lemon juice
1/4 teaspoon hot red pepper sauce

Mix the water, one can broth, the half-and-half and 3/4 teaspoon salt in a saucepan. Bring to a boil. Add the grits gradually, whisking constantly until blended. Reduce the heat and simmer for 10 minutes or until thickened, stirring occasionally. Stir in the Cheddar cheese, Parmesan cheese, butter, 1/2 teaspoon hot sauce and the white pepper. Remove from the heat and keep warm.

Cook the bacon in a skillet until crisp; drain, reserving 1 tablespoon of the drippings in the skillet. Crumble the bacon and set aside.

Season the shrimp with 1/8 teaspoon salt and the black pepper. Dredge in the flour, shaking off any excess. Sauté the mushrooms in the reserved drippings in the skillet for 5 minutes or until tender. Add the green onions and sauté for 2 minutes. Add the shrimp and garlic and sauté for 2 minutes or until the shrimp are light brown. Add 1/2 cup broth, the lemon juice and 1/4 teaspoon hot sauce. Cook for 2 minutes, stirring constantly and scraping up any brown bits from the bottom of the skillet. Serve over the hot grits. Sprinkle with the bacon. Serve with lemon wedges.

SERVES 4

Gump's Shrimp Creole

The Junior Auxiliary of Eastern Shore, Alabama, includes this recipe in the chapter's cookbook, Bay Seasons. *The JA of Eastern Shore presents* Puppets, *a child abuse prevention program, to students from kindergarten through third grade.*

SHRIMP STOCK
2 quarts water
1 onion, chopped
1 rib celery, chopped
Heads and shells from
   2 1/2 pounds shrimp

SHRIMP CREOLE
2 1/2 cups chopped onions
2 tablespoons vegetable oil
1 1/2 cups chopped celery
1 1/2 cups chopped green
   bell peppers
2 tablespoons butter
3 garlic cloves, minced

1 teaspoon hot red pepper sauce
1 bay leaf
2 teaspoons dried thyme
1 teaspoon salt
1 teaspoon black pepper
1/2 teaspoon dried basil
1/2 teaspoon cayenne pepper
1/2 cup Shrimp Stock
6 tomatoes, peeled and
   finely chopped
1 (15-ounce) can tomato sauce
1 1/2 cups Shrimp Stock
2 1/2 pounds shrimp, peeled
Hot cooked rice

To prepare the stock, combine the water, onion, celery, shrimp heads and shrimp shells in a large saucepan or stockpot. Bring to a simmer and simmer for 1 to 4 hours, adding water as needed to maintain 4 cups liquid. Strain the stock, discarding the solids. Use immediately or chill, covered, until needed.

To prepare the shrimp creole, sauté the onions in the oil for 3 to 4 minutes. Add the celery, bell peppers and butter. Sauté until tender. Stir in the garlic, hot sauce, bay leaf, thyme, salt, black pepper, basil and cayenne pepper. Reduce the heat to medium and add 1/2 cup of the stock. Cook for 5 minutes. Reduce the heat to low and stir in the tomatoes. Simmer for 15 minutes. Stir in the tomato sauce and 1 1/2 cups of the stock. Simmer for 30 minutes or until thick, stirring occasionally. Add the shrimp and cook until the shrimp turn pink, stirring frequently. Discard the bay leaf. Spoon over hot cooked rice.

SERVES 6 TO 8

Coming together is a beginning; keeping together is progress; working together is success!

—NAJA CROWNLET, 1953

Bacon-Wrapped Scallops with Lemon Chive Sauce

THE BUTCHER, THE BAKER AND THE COOKIE MAKER *is the cookbook of the Junior Auxiliary of Phillips County, Arkansas. The JA of Phillips County provides books for newborns with the* BOOKS FOR BABES *project.*

1 pound bacon
36 sea scallops
   (about 2 pounds)
2 tablespoons chopped fresh chives

2 tablespoons olive oil
2 tablespoons lemon juice
1/4 teaspoon salt
1/4 teaspoon pepper

Cut the bacon into halves crosswise. Wrap each scallop with a piece of the bacon and secure each with a wooden pick. Place on a rack in a broiler pan. Whisk the chives, olive oil, lemon juice, salt and pepper in a bowl until blended. Brush over the bacon-wrapped scallops. Broil 6 inches from the heat source until cooked to the desired degree of doneness. Serve immediately.

SERVES 6 TO 8

Crawfish Étouffée

1 large onion, chopped
1 bell pepper, chopped
2 or 3 ribs celery, chopped
1/2 cup (1 stick) butter
1 pound crawfish tails
Seasoning salt to taste

Creole seasoning to taste
1 to 2 tablespoons cornstarch
1/2 cup warm water
Chopped green onions
Hot cooked rice (optional)

Sauté the onion, bell pepper and celery in the butter in a skillet or saucepan until tender. Add the crawfish. Season with seasoning salt and Creole seasoning. Cook for 10 minutes or until the crawfish begin to curl, stirring frequently; remove from the heat. Dissolve the cornstarch in the warm water in a bowl. Stir into the crawfish. Return to low heat. Simmer for 3 to 4 minutes, stirring constantly. Stir in green onions just before serving. Serve over hot cooked rice. Shrimp may be substituted for the crawfish tails. Cook until the shrimp turn pink.

SERVES 4 TO 6

Crawfish Creole

1 1/2 cups chopped onions
1 cup chopped celery
1 bunch scallions, chopped
1 teaspoon minced garlic
1/2 cup (1 stick) butter
2/3 cup all-purpose flour
2 (15-ounce) cans tomato sauce
3 1/2 cups hot water
1/2 (15-ounce) jar mild picante
   sauce, or to taste

4 teaspoons sugar
2 bay leaves
1 teaspoon thyme
Salt and pepper to taste
2 (1-pound) packages fresh or
   frozen crawfish tails
1/4 cup parsley
3 cups hot cooked rice

Sauté the onions, celery, scallions and garlic in the butter in a skillet until tender. Add the flour and cook for 3 to 4 minutes, stirring constantly. Do not burn. Stir in the tomato sauce and water. Cook over medium heat. Stir in the picante sauce, sugar, bay leaves and thyme. Season with salt and pepper. Bring to a simmer, stirring constantly. Reduce the heat to low. Simmer, covered, for 30 minutes, stirring occasionally. Stir in the crawfish and parsley. Cook for 5 minutes or until the crawfish tails begin to curl. Spoon over the rice. Shrimp may be substituted for the crawfish. Cook until the shrimp turn pink.

SERVES 8

Oyster Casserole

3 cups oysters, drained
1 bunch green onions, chopped
1 rib celery, chopped
1/2 teaspoon Tabasco sauce
1 teaspoon Worcestershire sauce

1/2 cup (1 stick) butter, sliced
3 sleeves saltines, crushed
1 (12-ounce) can evaporated milk
1/2 cup half-and-half

Mix the oysters, green onions, celery, Tabasco sauce and Worcestershire sauce in a bowl. Layer the oyster mixture, butter and crackers in a baking dish. Mix the evaporated milk and half-and-half in a bowl and pour over the crackers. Bake at 375 degrees for 30 minutes or until bubbly.

SERVES 6

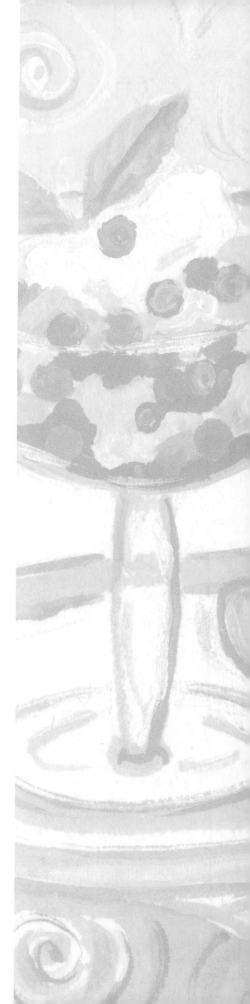

Oysters 2-2-2-2

16 fresh oysters, or 1 (16-ounce) jar
fresh raw oysters, drained, and
16 oyster half shells (see Note)

OYSTERS BIENVILLE
2 tablespoons butter
2 tablespoons all-purpose flour
1 (4-ounce) can small shrimp
4 or 5 large mushrooms, chopped
1/4 cup (1 ounce) grated
Parmesan cheese
1/4 cup white wine or milk,
or as needed
Salt and pepper to taste
Bread crumbs
Paprika to taste

OYSTERS ROCKEFELLER
1 cup frozen spinach, thawed and
drained
1/2 teaspoon anise extract
1/4 cup Bienville Sauce
(see method below)
1/4 cup plain or Italian
bread crumbs

1/4 cup (1 ounce) grated
Parmigiano-Rggiano cheese
1 dash of Worcestershire sauce
Salt to taste
Parmesan-Romano cheese

OYSTERS ROMA
1/2 cup Italian bread crumbs
1/2 cup (2 ounces) grated
Parmigiano-Rggiano cheese
1 tablespoon finely chopped garlic
1 tablespoon chopped fresh basil
1 green onion (green part only),
chopped
3 tablespoons (about) olive oil

OYSTERS MONTEREY
4 teaspoons mild Mexican salsa
with corn and beans
4 teaspoons masa
4 to 6 tablespoons shredded sharp
Cheddar cheese or pepper
Jack cheese

To shuck the oysters, wear a clean heavy-duty utility glove on your nondominant hand or hold a thick towel. Place an oyster with the curved half of the shell resting against the palm of your protected hand and the hinge pointing toward you. Hold the oyster firmly. Point the blade of an oyster knife (a special short wide-bladed knife) away from your body and insert it into the hinge of the oyster. Slowly rotate the knife clockwise until the upper shell comes loose. Remove the upper half shell completely from the curved bottom half shell. Use the blade of the oyster knife to carefully separate the oyster from the shell. Reserve the oyster and the curved bottom half shell. Discard the top half shell. Repeat with the remaining oysters.

Spray the smooth inside of the deep half shells with nonstick cooking spray and arrange smooth side up in two baking dishes. Place an oyster on each shell. Broil 4 to 6 inches from the heat source until the edges of the oysters begin to curl; set aside.

To prepare the Oysters Bienville, melt the butter in a 1-quart saucepan. Add the flour and cook over medium heat until the roux begins to turn light brown, stirring constantly. Stir in the undrained shrimp, mushrooms and cheese. If the sauce is too thick, add the wine gradually, stirring constantly until combined. Season with salt and pepper. Spoon over four of the oysters, reserving about 1/4 cup in the saucepan. Sprinkle the prepared oysters with bread crumbs and paprika.

To prepare the Oysters Rockefeller, add the spinach and anise extract to the reserved Bienville Sauce in the saucepan. Cook until heated through, stirring constantly. Stir in the bread crumbs, cheese and Worcestershire sauce. Season with salt. The sauce will be slightly crumbly. Spoon over four of the oysters. Sprinkle with additional cheese.

To prepare the Oysters Roma, combine the bread crumbs, cheese, garlic, basil and green onion in the saucepan. Add the olive oil gradually, stirring constantly until the mixture holds together and is slightly crumbly. Spoon over four of the oysters.

To prepare the Oysters Monterey, spoon 1 teaspoon salsa over the four remaining oysters. Sprinkle each with 1 teaspoon masa and the grated cheese.

The oysters may be assembled in advance. Chill, covered, until baking time. Bake all the oysters at 400 degrees for 15 to 20 minutes or until the tops begin to brown. Serve with a tossed green salad and crusty bread as a meal or serve alone as an appetizer. This recipe may be doubled or tripled.

Note: Oyster shells can be found at seafood processing facilities. Select the flat-bottomed deep half shells. Before using the oyster shells for the first time, scrub the shells clean and boil in water in a saucepan for 20 minutes. Drain and let the shells dry on a clean dish towel. These shells can be used over and over, saving you the time of shucking your own oysters each time. For easy cleanup after serving, oyster shells may be washed in a dishwasher basket in a dishwasher.

SERVES 2 TO 4

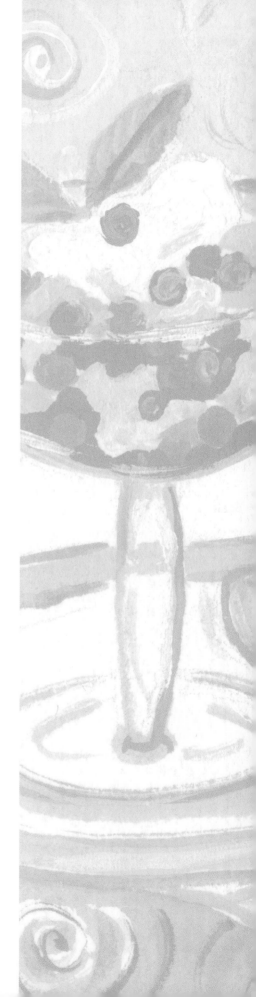

AWARD WINNER:

WARDROBE ROUNDUP—

JA OF RANKIN COUNTY

In the mid-1950s,

developmental psychologist

Abraham Maslow introduced

his theory that a person is

unable to reach his greatest

potential until his primary

needs are met. Although the

parents of many children

in Rankin County were

able to provide food, water,

and shelter, they were not

able financially to furnish

adequate clothing. In 1995,

the Junior Auxiliary of

Rankin County partnered

with Rankin County Human

Resource Agency to begin

Wardrobe Roundup to help

meet clothing needs of

poverty-level children in

grades K–12.

Salmon Croquettes

This recipe is from the Junior Auxiliary of Rankin County, Mississippi. The JA of Rankin County established the TEDDY BEAR CLINIC *to help overcome the fears of children who must visit the emergency room of a local hospital.*

1 (14-ounce) can salmon	1/2 teaspoon Creole seasoning
1 small onion, grated	1/2 teaspoon pepper
1 egg, lightly beaten	2 cups ranch-flavored croutons
3 tablespoons horseradish sauce	Vegetable oil for frying

Drain the salmon. Remove any bones and skin from the salmon and flake with a fork. Mix the salmon, onion, egg, horseradish sauce, Creole seasoning and pepper in a bowl. Place the croutons in a sealable plastic bag. Crush carefully with a rolling pin. Stir 3/4 cup crushed croutons into the salmon mixture. Shape into six patties. Coat with the remaining crushed croutons. Chill, covered, for 30 minutes. Fry in hot oil in a deep skillet until brown.

SERVES 6

Baked Cajun Catfish

2 cups cornmeal	2 tablespoons Cajun seasoning
2 teaspoons salt	1 to 2 teaspoons seasoning salt
1 tablespoon pepper	1/4 cup (1/2 stick) butter or
8 (3- to 4-ounce) catfish fillets	margarine, melted

Mix the cornmeal, salt and pepper in a shallow dish. Dredge the catfish in the cornmeal mixture, shaking off any excess. Place skin side down on a greased baking sheet. Mix the Cajun seasoning and seasoning salt in a bowl and sprinkle over the catfish. Drizzle with the butter. Bake at 400 degrees for 30 minutes or until the catfish is golden brown and begins to flake. Garnish with lemon slices.

SERVES 4

Trout Adele

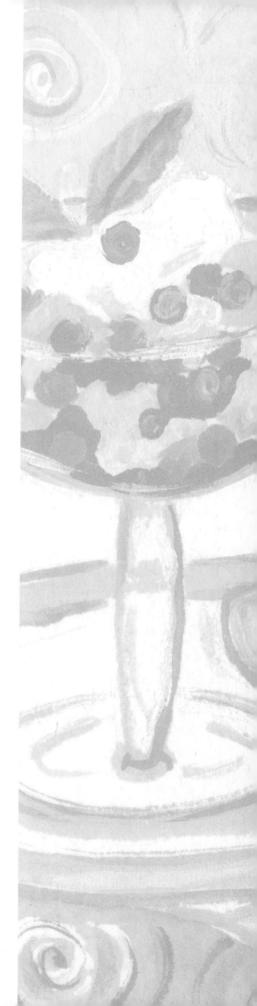

STUFFING
1/2 cup chopped onion
1/2 cup chopped bell pepper
1/2 cup chopped celery
1/2 cup chopped green onions
1/2 cup (1 stick) butter
4 ounces shrimp, peeled, deveined
  and chopped
1 pound jumbo lump crab meat
1/2 cup seasoned bread crumbs
1/4 cup plain bread crumbs
Salt and pepper to taste

SAUCE
1/4 cup chopped onion
1/4 cup chopped celery

1/4 cup chopped green onions
3 large garlic cloves, minced
1/2 cup (1 stick) butter
6 ounces shrimp, peeled
  and deveined
8 ounces mushrooms, sliced
1/2 cup white wine
1 teaspoon all-purpose flour

ASSEMBLY
14 to 16 trout fillets
1/4 cup (1/2 stick) butter, melted
Juice of 1 lemon
1 tablespoon chopped parsley

To prepare the stuffing, sauté the onion, bell pepper, celery and green onions in the butter in a skillet until tender. Add the shrimp and sauté until the shrimp turn pink. Fold in the crab meat and cook until heated through. Remove from the heat and fold in the seasoned bread crumbs and plain bread crumbs. Season with salt and pepper; set aside.

To prepare the sauce, sauté the onion, celery, green onions and garlic in the butter until tender. Add the shrimp and sauté until the shrimp turn pink. Stir in the mushrooms and wine. Simmer for 5 to 10 minutes. Whisk in the flour. Cook until thickened, whisking constantly. Keep warm.

To assemble, arrange half the trout in a 9×13-inch baking dish. Top each with a scoop of the stuffing and another trout fillet. Drizzle with the butter and lemon juice. Sprinkle with the parsley. Bake at 350 degrees for 45 minutes or until the fish begins to flake. Pour the sauce over the fish just before serving. This dish does not freeze well.

SERVES 6 TO 8

Desserts

Hurricanes Camille and Katrina

"Through the high winds and wild weather . . . it brought a bunch of us together." NAJA, through the years, has weathered storms of change, but none as significant as Hurricanes Camille and Katrina. Both of these catastrophic events destroyed homes, lives, and livelihoods on the coasts of Louisiana, Mississippi, and Alabama, and included in their victims JA members and chapters.

When Camille struck in 1969, the Association quickly rallied to unite the membership to aid the chapters and their communities that were in the path of destruction. Support flooded the coast. An Encouragement Fund was established to receive funds for distribution to chapters to assist them with the projects that were focused on the massive recovery effort. Then, in 2005, history repeated itself with devastating similarity when Katrina slammed into those same coastal communities, once again destroying the way of life of the residents—and galvanizing JA into action. ➤

Immediately, NAJA looked back at the precedent set during Camille and, with a precision born of experience, united the Association to reach out, meshing individual communities of service to embrace the entire coast as the NAJA service area. The Encouragement Fund was re-established to accept donations from chapters and individuals for aid to the area. NAJA encouraged chapters, businesses, schools, and individuals to send backpacks, uniforms, supplies, and books to reopen schools as soon as possible. Chapters adopted sister chapters on the coast and sent necessary materials to ensure that projects begun before the storm, as well as afterwards, continued.

And at Christmas, JA members planned and carried out a mass toy delivery to the area so that the children would still have magic in their lives. Even JA members who themselves were victims of the storms worked side by side to continue their legacy of service to others in need. The power of the winds of both Camille and Katrina left undeniable devastation in their paths, but the power of commitment to a common good remained unshaken. Those terrible winds only strengthened the bonds of dedication of the members of Junior Auxiliary to make a difference—and make a difference they did.

Coconut Cake with Divinity Frosting

CAKE

3 1/2 cups sifted cake flour
4 teaspoons baking powder
1/2 teaspoon salt
1 cup (2 sticks) unsalted
   butter, softened
2 cups sugar
1 cup milk
1 teaspoon almond extract
1 teaspoon coconut extract
1 cup freshly shredded coconut
8 extra-large egg whites

DIVINITY FROSTING

3 extra-large egg whites
1/8 teaspoon cream of tartar
1 dash of salt
3 cups sugar
1 cup hot water
1/4 cup light corn syrup
2 teaspoons almond extract

ASSEMBLY

3 (about) small coconuts, shredded
1 cup chopped fresh pineapple

To prepare the cake, sift the flour, baking powder and salt together twice. Cream the butter and sugar in a mixing bowl until light and fluffy. Add the sifted dry ingredients and milk alternately one-third at a time, mixing well after each addition. Beat in the almond extract, coconut extract and coconut. Beat the egg whites in a mixing bowl until stiff peaks form. Fold into the batter. Spoon into three greased and floured 9-inch cake pans. Bake at 375 degrees for 25 minutes.

To prepare the frosting, beat the egg whites, cream of tartar and salt in a mixing bowl until stiff peaks form. Combine the sugar, water and corn syrup in a saucepan. Bring to a boil. Cook over high heat to 270 to 290 degrees on a candy thermometer, soft crack-stage. Add half the hot syrup gradually to the egg white mixture, beating constantly at high speed. Bring the remaining syrup mixture to a boil. Add to the egg white mixture gradually, beating constantly at high speed. Add the almond extract. Beat at high speed until thick.

To assemble, place one cake layer on a cake plate. Spread the frosting over the layer and sprinkle with some of the coconut and half the pineapple. Top with another cake layer. Spread the top with the frosting and sprinkle with some of the coconut and the remaining pineapple. Top with the remaining cake layer. Secure with wooden dowels. Spread the remaining frosting over the top and side of the cake. Press the remaining coconut generously over top and around the side of the cake.

SERVES 12

Brown Mountain Cake

The favorite cookbook of the members of the Junior Auxiliary of Russellville, Arkansas, is their own, Among Friends. *JA of Russellville members taught etiquette lessons to children in the* Little Ladies/Little Lads *project.*

CAKE
1 cup (2 sticks) butter or
    margarine, softened
2 cups sugar
3 eggs
3 cups all-purpose flour
1 cup buttermilk
1/2 cup warm water
3 tablespoons baking cocoa

1 teaspoon baking soda
1 teaspoon vanilla extract

CARAMEL FROSTING
1 cup (2 sticks) butter
2 cups sugar
1 cup evaporated milk
1 teaspoon vanilla extract

To prepare the cake, beat the butter in a mixing bowl until light and fluffy. Add the sugar gradually, beating constantly. Cream until light and fluffy. Add the eggs one at a time, mixing well after each addition. Add the flour alternately with the buttermilk, beginning and ending with the flour and blending well after each addition. Mix the water, baking cocoa and baking soda in a bowl. Beat into the flour mixture. Stir in the vanilla. Pour into two greased and floured 9-inch cake pans. Bake at 350 degrees for 35 to 40 minutes or until a wooden pick inserted in the center comes out clean. Cool in the pans for 10 minutes. Remove to a wire rack to cool completely.

To prepare the frosting, melt the butter in a saucepan over medium heat. Stir in the sugar and evaporated milk. Cook over medium heat to 234 to 240 degrees on a candy thermometer, soft-ball stage. Remove from the heat and add the vanilla; do not stir. Let stand for 10 minutes. Beat at medium speed in a mixing bowl for 10 minutes or until thickened to a spreading consistency. Spread between the layers and over the top and side of the cake.

SERVES 12

"Years ago, we had at least two candidates for office at the elections held during our annual meetings, and the campaign slogans and 'give-aways' were great fun. Candidates actually had campaign chairmen! The best part was that if a chapter had a candidate in the election, their membership turned out in droves at the annual meeting. We had wonderful candidates every year, and the campaign speeches were phenomenal! Everyone was a 'winner.'"

—ANN GUICE
NAJA PRESIDENT,
1981–1982

Gingered Carrot Cake with Orange Cream Cheese Frosting

Cake
2 cups all-purpose flour
2 cups sugar
2 teaspoons baking powder
$1/2$ teaspoon baking soda
4 eggs, beaten
3 cups finely shredded carrots
$3/4$ cup vegetable oil
$3/4$ cup dried fruit bits
$3/4$ teaspoon ginger

Orange Cream Cheese Frosting
6 ounces cream cheese, softened
$1/2$ cup (1 stick) butter, softened
1 teaspoon orange juice
$41/2$ to $43/4$ cups confectioners' sugar
$1/2$ teaspoon finely grated orange zest
1 cup finely chopped pecans

To prepare the cake, mix the flour, sugar, baking powder and baking soda in a large bowl. Mix the eggs, carrots, oil, dried fruit and ginger in a bowl. Stir into the flour mixture. Pour into two 9-inch cake pans. Bake at 350 degrees for 30 to 35 minutes or until a wooden pick inserted in the center comes out clean. Cool in the pans on a wire rack for 10 minutes. Remove to a wire rack to cool completely.

To prepare the frosting, beat the cream cheese and butter in a mixing bowl until light and fluffy. Beat in the orange juice. Add the confectioners' sugar gradually, beating constantly. Beat until the frosting thickens to a spreading consistency. Stir in the orange zest. Spread between the layers and over the top and side of the cake. Sprinkle with the pecans.

Serves 12 to 15

Red Velvet Cake with Fluffy White Frosting

The Junior Auxiliary of Corinth, Mississippi, submitted this recipe. The JA of Corinth mentors special-needs children in the BUILDING BUTTERFLIES *project, the 2007 Louise Eskrigge Crump Award-winner.*

CAKE
1/2 cup (1 stick) butter, softened
1 1/2 cups sugar
1 teaspoon vanilla extract
2 eggs
2 teaspoons (heaping) baking cocoa
3 drops of red food coloring
2 1/2 cups cake flour
1 teaspoon salt
1 cup buttermilk

1 tablespoon vinegar
1 teaspoon baking soda

FLUFFY WHITE FROSTING
6 tablespoons all-purpose flour
2 cups milk
2 cups (4 sticks) butter, softened
2 cups sugar
1 teaspoon vanilla extract

To prepare the cake, cream the butter, sugar and vanilla in a mixing bowl until light and fluffy. Add the eggs one at a time, beating well after each addition. Mix the baking cocoa and food coloring in a bowl. This will make a thick paste. Beat into the creamed mixture. Mix the flour and salt together. Add the flour mixture and buttermilk alternately 1 tablespoon at a time to the creamed mixture, beginning and ending with the flour mixture and beating well after each addition. Mix the vinegar and baking soda in a bowl. Beat into the batter. Spoon into two greased and floured 8-inch cake pans. Bake at 350 degrees for 20 to 30 minutes or until a wooden pick inserted in the center comes out clean. Let cool completely.

To prepare the frosting, mix the flour and enough milk to make a thick paste in the top of a double boiler. Place over simmering water. Add the remaining milk gradually, stirring constantly. Cook until thickened, stirring constantly. Let stand until cool. Cream the butter and sugar in a mixing bowl until light and fluffy. Beat in the vanilla. Add the milk mixture gradually, beating constantly until firm peaks form. Spread between the layers and over the top and side of the cake.

SERVES 12

Since 1941, the President has served as the chief executive officer of NAJA, responding to the needs of the Association, directing programs, interpreting policy, coordinating activities, and traveling throughout the JA community. In 1985, NAJA created Crown and Gavel, an honorary society of past presidents, in an effort to harness their vast knowledge and expertise to have it available if counsel was needed. They are honored each year at the annual meeting of NAJA.

Decorator Cake and Decorator Icing

CAKE
1 (2-layer) package white cake mix
1/2 cup sugar
3/4 cup vegetable oil or olive oil
1 cup sour cream, buttermilk or a
  combination of sour cream and
  buttermilk
4 eggs, or 2 eggs plus 3 egg whites
1/2 teaspoon vanilla extract plus
  1/2 teaspoon almond extract, or
  1 tablespoon other flavoring

DECORATOR ICING
2 (1-pound) packages
  confectioners' sugar
3/4 cup white cake mix
1 cup shortening
3/4 cup (about) water
1 teaspoon almond extract

To prepare the cake, beat the cake mix, sugar, oil, sour cream, eggs and vanilla mixture in a mixing bowl for 10 minutes. Spoon into a 9×13-inch cake pan, two 9-inch cake pans or a 12-cup bundt pan. Bake at 325 degrees for 30 to 35 minutes. The cake will not rise much.

To prepare the icing, mix the confectioners' sugar, cake mix, shortening, water and almond extract in a bowl until smooth. Use less water for making flowers and borders. Use more water for spreading smoothly between the layers and over the top and side of the cake.

SERVES 10 TO 12

Banana Pudding Cake

1 or 2 small bananas, mashed
1 (2-layer) package yellow cake mix
1 (4-ounce) package banana cream
  instant pudding mix

4 eggs
1 cup water
1/4 cup vegetable oil
1/2 cup chopped pecans (optional)

Combine the bananas, cake mix, pudding mix, eggs, water and oil in a mixing bowl. Beat for 2 minutes. Stir in the pecans. Pour into a bundt pan heavily sprayed with nonstick cooking spray. Bake at 350 degrees for 1 hour or until the cake tests done. Cool in the pan for 30 to 40 minutes or until the cake is barely warm. Invert onto a serving plate. Frozen bananas may be used once thawed. This cake freezes well.

SERVES 10 TO 12

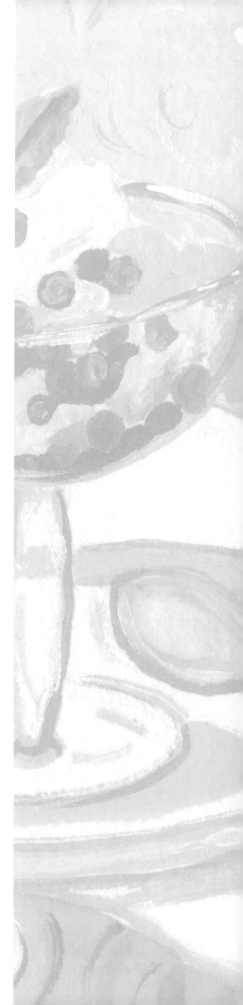

Strawberry Daiquiri Cake

1 (2-layer) package strawberry
   cake mix
1 (5-ounce) can evaporated milk

1 (10-ounce) can frozen strawberry
   daiquiri mix, thawed
8 ounces whipped topping

Prepare the cake mix according to the package directions. Bake in a greased and floured 9×13-inch cake pan. Pierce the top of the warm cake all over. Pour the evaporated milk evenly over the cake and let stand for 3 to 4 minutes or until most of the liquid is absorbed. Pour the daiquiri mix evenly over the cake and let stand until the liquids are absorbed. Spread the whipped topping evenly over the top. Chill, covered, for 8 to 10 hours. For a variation, add sliced strawberries to the whipped topping.

SERVES 8 TO 10

Apple Crumb Pie

The Junior Auxiliary of Independence County, Arkansas, donated this recipe. The JA of Independence County conducts a year-round reading program at the local library in the READING MAKES YOU GROW *project.*

PIE
2¹/2 pounds large baking apples
   (about 3 or 4)
¹/2 cup sugar
2 tablespoons all-purpose flour
¹/2 teaspoon cinnamon
1 unbaked (9-inch) pie shell
2 tablespoons lemon juice

TOPPING
¹/2 cup sugar
¹/2 cup all-purpose flour
¹/2 cup (1 stick) butter, softened

To prepare the pie, peel, core and quarter the apples. Slice the quarters into halves crosswise. Mix the apples, sugar, flour and cinnamon in a bowl. Spoon into the pie shell and sprinkle with the lemon juice.

To prepare the topping, mix the sugar, flour and butter in a bowl until crumbly. Sprinkle over the pie. Slide the pie into a heavy-duty nonrecycled paper bag. Fold down the end and secure with paper clips. Place on a baking sheet. Bake at 425 degrees for 1 hour. Be sure that the paper bag is not touching any of the heating elements. Split the bag in half and remove the pie. Let stand until cool. This recipe is not recommended for gas ovens.

SERVES 6 TO 8

Key Lime Pie

GRAHAM CRACKER CRUST
1 cup graham cracker crumbs
1/4 cup (1/2 stick) butter, melted
1 tablespoon sugar
1 1/2 teaspoons cinnamon

FILLING
5 egg yolks
1 (14-ounce) can sweetened
  condensed milk
Juice of 6 to 8 Key limes (about
  2/3 cup), or bottled Key lime juice
Fresh whipped cream

To prepare the crust, mix the graham cracker crumbs, butter, sugar and cinnamon in a bowl. Press over the bottom and up the side of a 9-inch pie plate. Bake at 325 degrees for 8 minutes. Let stand until cool.

To prepare the filling, process the egg yolks in a food processor fitted with a metal blade or beat in a mixing bowl for 2 minutes. Add the condensed milk and process until combined. Add the lime juice and process for 2 minutes. Pour into the pie shell. Bake at 325 degrees for 10 to 15 minutes or until the center is set. Cool on a wire rack for 1 hour. Chill, covered with plastic wrap, for 3 to 10 hours. Top with whipped cream.

SERVES 6 TO 8

Pecan Pie

The Junior Auxiliary of Nashville, Arkansas, submitted this recipe. The JA of Nashville hosts Thanksgiving dinner for needy families in the community with the BASKET OF THANKS *project.*

2 tablespoons all-purpose flour
1/2 cup sugar
3 eggs, lightly beaten
1 cup light corn syrup
1/3 cup butter, melted

1 teaspoon vanilla extract
1 cup pecans
1 unbaked (9-inch) deep-dish
  pie shell

Mix the flour and sugar in a bowl. Add the eggs, corn syrup, butter and vanilla. Blend until smooth. Stir in the pecans. Spoon into the pie shell. Bake at 350 degrees for 45 to 50 minutes or until the center is firm.

SERVES 6 TO 8

Elegant Strawberry Pie

1/2 cup (1 stick) margarine, melted
1/4 cup packed brown sugar
1 cup sifted all-purpose flour
1/2 cup chopped pecans
1 1/2 cups strawberries, crushed
1 cup granulated sugar
2 egg whites
2 tablespoons lemon juice
1 cup heavy whipping cream, whipped

Mix the margarine, brown sugar, flour and pecans in a bowl. Spread out on a baking sheet. Bake at 325 degrees for 20 minutes. Cool on the baking sheet. Crumble and spread over the bottom and up the side of two 9-inch pie plates, reserving 1/2 cup of the crumbs. Combine the strawberries, granulated sugar, egg whites and lemon juice in a mixing bowl. Beat at low speed for 30 minutes or until soft peaks form. Fold in the whipped cream. Spoon into the pie shells. Sprinkle with the reserved crumbs. Freeze, covered, until set. Let the pies stand at room temperature for 5 to 10 minutes before slicing. Garnish with sliced strawberries.

SERVES 12 TO 16

Baked Caramel Custard

1 cup sugar
6 eggs
1/2 cup sugar
1 teaspoon vanilla extract
1/8 teaspoon salt
4 cups milk

Cook 1 cup sugar in a saucepan over medium heat until the sugar has melted and begins to turn light brown. Pour into a 2-quart mold. Turn and rotate the mold until the bottom and side is coated with the caramel. Beat the eggs in a mixing bowl until smooth. Add 1/2 cup sugar, the vanilla and salt. Beat until combined. Heat the milk in a saucepan until bubbles form around the edge. Add to the egg mixture gradually, beating constantly until combined. Pour into the mold.

Place the mold in a larger baking pan. Add hot water to the larger baking pan to a depth of 1/2 inch. Bake at 325 degrees for 50 minutes or until a knife inserted in the center comes out clean. Remove the mold from the larger baking pan and let stand until completely cool. Chill, covered, until serving time. Invert into a shallow baking dish or onto a serving plate. Spoon any caramel left in the pan over the top of the custard and serve as a sauce.

SERVES 6

He had grown up with no mother, a handicapped father, and an outhouse. However, with determination and the help of JA, not only did he finish college, but he completed his Master's Degree. He brought his sons to meet me and said, "I want them to know that if anything ever happens to me, you and your ladies will take care of them."

—PROJECT RICKY

Fabulous Apple Dumplings

1 (2-crust) pie pastry
6 apples
$1/2$ cup sugar
$1^1/2$ teaspoons cinnamon
2 tablespoons margarine

1 cup sugar
2 cups water
3 tablespoons margarine
$1/4$ teaspoon cinnamon

Roll each pastry into a $1/8$-inch-thick rectangle. Cut each into 7-inch squares. Peel and core the apples. Place one apple in the center of each of the pastry squares. Combine $1/2$ cup sugar and $1^1/2$ teaspoons cinnamon in a bowl and mix well. Spoon into the apples, filling the cored cavities. Top each with 1 teaspoon of the margarine. Pull the opposite corners of the pastry up and over the apples, overlapping the corners. Moisten with a small amount of water to seal. Repeat with the opposite corners of the pastry. Arrange in a baking dish. Do not let the apples touch.

Mix 1 cup sugar, the water, 3 tablespoons margarine and $1/4$ teaspoon cinnamon in a saucepan. Bring to a boil, stirring occasionally. Boil for 3 minutes. Pour around the bases of the apple dumplings. Bake at 400 degrees until the pastry is golden brown and the apples are tender, basting occasionally with the syrup. Serve warm with vanilla ice cream. For a variation, substitute peaches for the apples.

SERVES 6

Brown Sugar Peaches

3 pounds peaches
Juice of 2 lemons
$1/4$ cup packed brown sugar

$1/4$ cup rum
1 cup heavy whipping cream
1 cup sour cream

Peel and slice the peaches. Toss with the lemon juice in a bowl. Add the brown sugar and rum. Toss until coated. Chill, covered, for 4 hours. Beat the whipping cream in a mixing bowl until soft peaks form. Fold in the sour cream. Chill, covered, until serving time. Serve the whipped cream mixture spooned over the top of the peaches.

SERVES 8 TO 10

"It was not by accident or whim, but rather with commitment to a mission, that we, in Association, chose to place particular emphasis on the welfare of children."

—NORMA DeLONG
RICHARDS, EXECUTIVE
DIRECTOR, 1994 BULLETIN

Poached Pears

1 cup water	1 cinnamon stick
1/2 cup port	2 cloves
1/4 cup sugar	2 lemon slices
1 tablespoon Poire Williams (pear-flavored brandy)	6 Anjou pears, peeled
	Warm chocolate sauce

Combine the water, port, sugar, Poire Williams, cinnamon stick, cloves and lemon slices in a large skillet or saucepan. Bring to a simmer. Stand the pears upright in the liquid. Simmer until the pears are tender; drain reserving the cooking syrup. Place each warm pear on a dessert plate and drizzle with the reserved cooking syrup and chocolate sauce.

SERVES 6

Bananas Foster

1/2 cup (1 stick) butter	1/2 cup white rum
2 cups packed brown sugar	1/2 cup crème de banana
1 teaspoon cinnamon	Vanilla ice cream
4 bananas, sliced 1/2 inch thick	

Melt the butter in a skillet over high heat. Add the brown sugar and stir until dissolved. Stir in the cinnamon. Bring to a boil, stirring constantly. Add the bananas and cook for 2 minutes or until tender. Add the rum and crème de banana carefully. Bring to a rapid boil. Dim the lights, if desired, for effect. Remove from the heat and carefully ignite the fumes near the top of the sauce with a long match. Flambé for 1 minute or until the flame subsides. Spoon over vanilla ice cream. Serve immediately.

SERVES 6

Cherry Berry on a Cloud

MERINGUE SHELL
6 egg whites
1/2 teaspoon cream of tartar
1/4 teaspoon salt
13/4 cups sugar

FILLING
8 ounces cream cheese, softened
1 cup sugar
1 teaspoon vanilla extract
2 cups miniature marshmallows

2 cups heavy whipping
    cream, whipped

SAUCE
1 (16-ounce) can cherry pie filling
1 teaspoon almond extract
1 teaspoon lemon juice
1 dash of salt
2 cups sliced strawberries, or
    1 (16-ounce) package frozen
    strawberries, thawed

To prepare the shell, beat the egg whites, cream of tartar and salt in a mixing bowl until foamy. Add the sugar gradually, beating constantly until combined. Beat for 15 minutes or until stiff peaks form. Spread in a 9×13-inch baking dish sprayed with nonstick cooking spray. Bake at 275 degrees for 1 hour. Turn off the oven. Let the shell stand in the closed oven for 12 hours.

To prepare the filling, mix the cream cheese, sugar and vanilla in a bowl. Fold in the marshmallows and whipped cream. Spread over the shell. Chill, covered, for 8 to 12 hours.

To prepare the sauce, mix the pie filling, almond extract, lemon juice and salt in a bowl. Fold in the strawberries. Chill until serving time. Slice the tart and place on dessert plates. Spoon the sauce over the top.

SERVES 6 TO 8

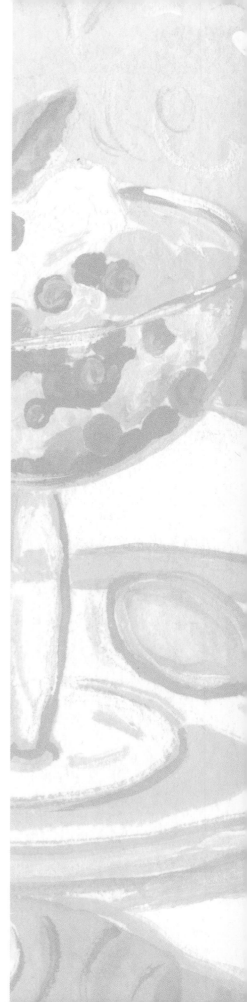

Orange Balls

The Junior Auxiliary of West Point, Mississippi, includes this recipe in Down Home. *The JA of West Point is a charter chapter of NAJA, a member since 1941.*

"For our first service project, the Provisional class of JA of West Point organized a dance for the children of Camp Rising Sun, a summer camp for children living with terminal illness. We chose a western theme and decorated the mess hall with hay bales, bandanas, saddles, boots, and spurs. Everyone danced the night away with the deejay! What a wonderful introduction into an organization that so greatly impacts the lives of children!"

—Active Member,
JA of West Point

1 (12-ounce) package vanilla
  wafers, crushed
1/2 cup (1 stick)
  margarine, softened
1 (6-ounce) can frozen orange juice
  concentrate, thawed

1 (1-pound) package
  confectioners' sugar
1 cup chopped pecans
1 (14-ounce) package
  shredded coconut

Mix the vanilla wafers, margarine, orange juice concentrate and confectioners' sugar in a bowl. Stir in the pecans. Shape into small balls and roll in the coconut. Store in an airtight container in the refrigerator.

Makes 4 to 5 dozen

Salted Peanut Chews

The Junior Auxiliary of Booneville, Mississippi, submitted the following recipe from the chapter's cookbook, Recipe Recollections. *The JA of Booneville received the MAG Award in 2007 for the project* Food and Mood.

1 (17-ounce) package peanut
  butter cookie mix
3 tablespoons vegetable oil
1 tablespoon water
1 egg, lightly beaten
3 cups miniature marshmallows
2/3 cup light corn syrup

1/4 cup (1/2 stick) butter
  or margarine
1 (10-ounce) package peanut
  butter chips
2 teaspoons vanilla extract
2 cups crisp rice cereal
2 cups salted peanuts

Mix the cookie mix, oil, water and egg in a bowl. Press over the bottom of a 9×13-inch baking dish sprayed with nonstick cooking spray. Bake at 350 degrees for 12 to 15 minutes or until firm. Sprinkle with the marshmallows immediately. Bake for 1 to 2 minutes longer or until the marshmallows begin to puff up.

Mix the corn syrup, butter, peanut butter chips and vanilla in a 4-quart saucepan. Cook over low heat until smooth, stirring frequently. Remove from the heat and stir in the cereal and peanuts. Spoon over the marshmallows immediately and spread to the edges of the baking pan. Chill, covered, for 30 minutes or until firm. Cut into bars.

Makes 2 dozen

Apricot Snowflakes

3 to 5 (16-ounce) packages
  dried apricots
1 (14-ounce) can sweetened
  condensed milk

1 cup chopped pecans
2 to 3 cups confectioners' sugar
1 (14-ounce) package shredded
  coconut or freshly shredded coconut

Process the apricots in a food processor until finely chopped. Mix the apricots, condensed milk and pecans in a bowl. Add the confectioners' sugar gradually until a firm dough forms, stirring constantly. Shape into small balls. Roll in the coconut. Store in an airtight container at room temperature for up to 10 days.

MAKES ABOUT 65 TO 75

Blueberry Crunch Cookies

1 (18-ounce) package blueberry
  muffin mix (with canned
  blueberries)
1 egg, lightly beaten
3/4 cup rolled oats

1/2 cup (1 stick) butter, softened
1/3 cup self-rising flour
1/3 cup granulated sugar
1/3 cup packed light brown sugar

Drain the blueberries, discarding the liquid. Combine the muffin mix, egg, oats, butter, flour, granulated sugar and brown sugar in a mixing bowl. Beat until combined. Fold in the blueberries. Drop by spoonfuls onto a cookie sheet. Bake at 350 degrees for 10 to 12 minutes.

MAKES 3 DOZEN

Praline Lace Cookies

1 1/2 cups pecans, chopped
1 cup sugar
1/4 cup all-purpose flour
1/3 teaspoon baking powder

1/8 teaspoon salt
1/2 cup (1 stick) butter, melted
1 egg, lightly beaten
2 teaspoons vanilla extract

Mix the pecans, sugar, flour, baking powder and salt in a bowl. Stir in the butter, egg and vanilla. Chill, covered, for 8 to 10 hours. Drop by teaspoonfuls 3 inches apart onto a foil-lined cookie sheet. Bake at 325 degrees for 10 to 12 minutes. Let cool slightly on the cookie sheet. Remove to a wire rack to cool completely. Be sure the cookie dough is well chilled before baking or the cookies will not set properly.

MAKES 3 TO 4 DOZEN

Quick Peanut Butter Cookies

1 egg, lightly beaten
1 cup sugar
1 cup creamy peanut butter

Mix the egg, sugar and peanut butter in a bowl. Drop by spoonfuls onto a lightly greased cookie sheet. Flatten with a fork. Bake at 350 degrees for 15 minutes.

Makes 2 dozen

Butter Melt-a-ways with Pink Frosting

The Junior Auxiliary of Conway, Arkansas, includes this recipe in the cookbook Simply Irresistible. *The JA of Conway teaches healthy lifestyles to girls in the* Girls Run Arkansas *project.*

Cookies
1 1/4 cups all-purpose flour
3/4 cup cornstarch
1/3 cup confectioners' sugar, plus
  more as needed
1 cup (2 sticks) butter, softened

Pink Frosting
3 ounces cream cheese, softened
1 cup confectioners' sugar
1/2 teaspoon vanilla extract
1/2 to 1 drop of red food coloring

To prepare the cookies, combine the flour, cornstarch, 1/3 cup confectioners' sugar and the butter in a mixing bowl. Beat until combined. Separate the dough into two equal portions. Roll each portion into a log on a waxed paper-lined surface dusted with additional confectioners' sugar. Chill, wrapped tightly in waxed paper, for 6 to 10 hours. Cut into slices and place on a greased cookie sheet. Bake at 350 degrees for 12 minutes. Cool on a wire rack.

To prepare the frosting, beat the cream cheese, confectioners' sugar, vanilla and food coloring in a mixing bowl until smooth. Drop a dollop of icing onto the center of each cookie.

For a variation, substitute Lemon Frosting. Beat 1/4 cup (1/2 stick) softened butter or margarine in a mixing bowl until light and fluffy. Gradually add 1 1/2 cups confectioners' sugar and 2 tablespoons lemon juice, beating constantly until combined. Cream until light and fluffy. Stir in 1 tablespoon grated lemon zest.

Makes 3 dozen

Award Winner:

Fitness Frenzy—

JA of Paragould

This project was started to bring awareness to the national epidemics of obesity, poor nutrition, unhealthy lifestyles, and the psychosocial effects of these circumstances in childhood. The project involved providing information and appropriate solutions for these issues, as well as allowing the youth who participated to receive free health screenings and services.

Caramel Cheesecake Bars

CHRISTMAS BLESSINGS, *a cookbook by the Junior Auxiliary of Paragould, Arkansas, includes this recipe. The JA of Paragould won the 2004 Martha Wise Award for* FITNESS FRENZY.

1 1/2 cups vanilla wafers, crushed
1/2 cup chopped pecans
1/4 cup (1/2 stick) butter, melted
32 ounces cream cheese, softened
1 cup sugar
1 cup sour cream

3 tablespoons all-purpose flour
1 tablespoon vanilla extract
4 eggs
1/2 cup chopped pecans
1/4 cup caramel topping

Line a 9×13-inch baking dish with foil, allowing extra foil on the ends. Fold the extra foil into handles. Grease the foil. Mix the vanilla wafers, 1/2 cup pecans and the butter in a bowl. Press over the bottom of the prepared dish. Chill, covered, until needed. Combine the cream cheese and sugar in a mixing bowl. Cream at medium speed until light and fluffy. Add the sour cream, flour and vanilla. Beat until smooth. Add the eggs one at a time, beating well at low speed after each addition. Pour into the crust. Bake at 325 degrees for 45 minutes. Chill, covered, for 4 hours. Lift out of the pan using the foil handles. Sprinkle with 1/2 cup pecans and drizzle with the caramel topping. Cut into bars.

MAKES 32

White Chocolate Gooey Butter Cake Squares

1 (2-layer) package yellow cake mix
1 egg
1/2 cup (1 stick) butter, melted
8 ounces cream cheese, softened
2 eggs
1 teaspoon vanilla extract

1 (1-pound) package
   confectioners' sugar
1/2 cup (1 stick) butter, melted
1 cup (6 ounces) white
   chocolate chips

Mix the cake mix, 1 egg and 1/2 cup butter in a bowl. Press over the bottom of a lightly greased 9×13-inch baking dish. Beat the cream cheese in a mixing bowl until smooth. Add 2 eggs and the vanilla. Beat until combined. Beat in the confectioners' sugar until combined. Add 1/2 cup butter gradually, mixing constantly at low speed until combined. Fold in the white chocolate chips. Spread over the cake mix layer. Bake at 350 degrees for 40 to 50 minutes. Do not overbake; the center should be slightly gooey. Let stand until cool. Cut into squares.

MAKES 2 DOZEN

Chocolate

Making a Difference

When I joined JA in 2002, I was looking for a way to get involved in my community. I wanted something where I could feel like I was making a difference on a personal level, and my chapter's Shoes for Souls project has really become my personal connection to what we do.

Living in an affluent community, it is so easy for people to think that there isn't need in our county. They couldn't be more wrong! There are children showing up to school with shoes that are too big, too small, full of holes, falling apart, and even a little brother wearing his big sister's hand-me-downs. ➤

That's where the Junior Auxiliary steps in with our Shoes for Souls project. We provide brand new pairs of athletic shoes to hundreds of children in need each year throughout our county. Working with the schools, we personally measure the kids' feet and deliver the shoes to them, making sure that they fit properly before we leave. When we do need to exchange a pair for a better fit, the kids beg us not to take the ones that we brought because they want them so badly. So many of these children have never had a new pair of shoes that were purchased just for them. Many of them didn't even know how a pair of shoes should fit them and would tell us that the shoes were too tight because all they knew were hand-me-downs that were too big. After telling them that they would be able to play sports without their shoes flying off, the kids just beamed.

This is one of the most rewarding projects my chapter has because of the opportunity to actually interact with the children who benefit. Giving them a pair of athletic shoes meets NAJA's National Focus, Healthy Children—Healthy Futures, because it enables them to participate on the playground. And we also have the opportunity to build up their emotional health by giving them a sense of pride and putting tremendous smiles on their faces!

But on a personal level, this is a project where I've been able to take my preschool-aged children along. The opportunity to let them see compassion in action and to educate them on how we can make a difference is priceless.

—THE JUNIOR AUXILIARY OF FRANKLIN

Chocolate Bread Pudding with Whiskey Sauce

BREAD PUDDING
1/4 cup (1/2 stick) unsalted butter
7 cups French bread cubes
2 cups whipping cream
1 cup milk
8 ounces bittersweet
   chocolate, chopped
5 egg yolks, lightly beaten
2/3 cup packed light brown sugar
1 teaspoon vanilla extract

WHISKEY SAUCE
3/4 cup milk
1/2 cup sugar
1/4 cup (1/2 stick) butter
2 tablespoons water
1 1/2 tablespoons cornstarch
1/4 cup bourbon

To prepare the bread pudding, melt the butter in a large heavy skillet over medium heat. Add the bread cubes and cook for 3 minutes or until golden brown, stirring constantly. Remove to a greased 9×13-inch baking dish.

Combine the whipping cream and milk in a saucepan. Bring to a boil. Remove from the heat and add the chocolate. Whisk until smooth. Add the egg yolks, brown sugar and vanilla. Whisk until smooth. Pour over the bread and let stand for 30 minutes. Cover with foil and poke six small holes in the foil to allow steam to escape. Place the baking dish in a larger baking pan. Add hot water to the larger pan to a depth of 1 1/2 inches. Bake at 325 degrees for 1 3/4 hours or until set. Let stand on a wire rack for 30 minutes.

To prepare the sauce, combine the milk, sugar and butter in a saucepan. Cook over low heat until the butter melts and the sugar dissolves, stirring frequently. Mix the water and cornstarch in a bowl until smooth. Add to the milk mixture and stir until combined. Stir in the bourbon. Bring to a boil over medium heat, stirring constantly. Boil for 2 minutes, stirring constantly. Serve with the warm bread pudding.

SERVES 8 TO 10

"When I joined Junior Auxiliary I found where I was supposed to be. This was my way to help all of the children I was never able to have of my own."

—ESTHER HERRING

Chocolate Cobbler

1 cup (2 sticks) margarine	1 teaspoon vanilla extract
1 1/2 cups self-rising flour	1 cup sugar
3/4 cup milk	6 tablespoons baking cocoa
1/2 cup sugar	1 1/2 cups water

Melt the margarine in a 9×13-inch baking dish. Mix the flour, milk, 1/2 cup sugar and the vanilla in a bowl. Pour into the baking dish. Mix 1 cup sugar and the baking cocoa. Sprinkle over the batter. Pour the water over the top; do not stir. Bake at 350 degrees for 30 minutes. Do not overcook. Serve with ice cream, if desired.

SERVES 8 TO 10

Chocolate Almond Torte

1 (23-ounce) package brownie mix with chocolate chips	1/4 cup baking cocoa
3 eggs	3 tablespoons water
1/4 cup water	2 tablespoons vegetable oil
1 cup heavy whipping cream	2 tablespoons light corn syrup
1/4 cup confectioners' sugar, sifted	2 cups confectioners' sugar, sifted
1/4 to 1/2 teaspoon almond extract	1/2 cup sliced almonds, toasted

Mix the brownie mix, eggs and 1/4 cup water in a bowl. Pour into three greased and floured 8-inch cake pans. Bake at 350 for 12 minutes. Cool in the pans on a wire rack for 10 minutes. Remove to the wire rack to cool completely.

Beat the whipping cream at medium speed in a mixing bowl until foamy. Add 1/4 cup confectioners' sugar gradually, mixing constantly until firm peaks form. Stir in the almond extract. Spread between the layers of the torte.

Combine the baking cocoa, 3 tablespoons water, the oil and corn syrup in a saucepan. Cook over low heat for 2 minutes or until smooth, stirring constantly. Remove from the heat and stir in 2 cups confectioners' sugar. Drizzle over the top of the torte. Sprinkle or decorate the top and side with the almonds.

SERVES 12

Chocolate Chip Cheesecake

A TASTE OF TISHOMINGO is the cookbook from the Junior Auxiliary of Tishomingo County, Mississippi. The JA of Tishomingo County's HELPING HAND project provides needed items such as class rings, prom attire, senior pictures, and graduation invitations for foster care students.

1 1/2 cups graham cracker crumbs
1/3 cup baking cocoa
1/3 cup sugar
1/3 cup butter or margarine, melted
24 ounces cream cheese, softened
1 (14-ounce) can sweetened
  condensed milk

3 eggs
2 teaspoons vanilla extract
1 cup miniature semisweet
  chocolate chips
1 teaspoon all-purpose flour

Mix the graham cracker crumbs, baking cocoa, sugar and butter in a bowl. Press evenly over the bottom of a 9-inch springform pan. Beat the cream cheese in a mixing bowl until light and fluffy. Add the condensed milk gradually, mixing constantly until smooth. Beat in the eggs and vanilla. Toss 1/2 cup of the chocolate chips with the flour in a bowl. Stir into the cream cheese mixture. Pour into the graham cracker shell. Sprinkle with the remaining 1/2 cup chocolate chips. Bake at 300 drgrees for 1 hour. Turn off the oven; do not remove the cheesecake. Let stand in the closed oven for 1 hour. Remove from the oven and let cool completely. Chill, covered, until serving time.

SERVES 10 TO 12

Toffee Tiramisu

1 (10-ounce) package frozen pound
  cake, thawed
3/4 cup strong brewed coffee
8 ounces cream cheese, softened
1 cup sugar

1/2 cup chocolate syrup
1 cup heavy whipping
  cream, whipped
2 (1.4-ounce) chocolate-covered
  toffee bars, crushed

Cut the cake into nine slices. Arrange in a 7×11-inch baking dish, cutting the pieces of cake as needed to fit in a single layer. Drizzle with the coffee. Beat the cream cheese and sugar in a mixing bowl until smooth. Add the chocolate syrup and beat until combined. Fold in the whipped cream. Spread over the pound cake layer. Sprinkle with the candy bars. Chill, covered, until serving time.

SERVES 8

Toffee Chocolate Pecan Pie

Following a devastating
tornado in 1938, the women
of Tupelo, Mississippi,
banded together to help
those in need. These women
called themselves the Tupelo
Service League. In 1951
TSL petitioned NAJA and
became the Junior Auxiliary
of Tupelo.

This recipe is from the Junior Auxiliary of Rogers-Bentonville, Arkansas.
The JA of Rogers-Bentonville selects one high-impact project in the
community to complete in one day with the DONE IN A DAY *project.*

4 ounces chocolate-covered toffee bars (about 3), chopped	1 cup light corn syrup
1 unbaked (9-inch) pie shell	1/2 cup sugar
4 eggs, lightly beaten	1 tablespoon vanilla extract
1/4 cup (1/2 stick) unsalted butter, melted	3/4 cup (4 1/2 ounces) semisweet chocolate chips
	1 cup pecans, coarsely chopped

Sprinkle the candy bars over the bottom of the pie shell. Mix the eggs, butter, corn syrup, sugar and vanilla in a bowl. Stir in the chocolate chips and pecans. Pour into the pie shell. Bake at 350 degrees for 50 to 55 minutes.

SERVES 6 TO 8

Chocolate Angel Pie

2 (24-count) packages frozen ladyfingers, thawed	6 to 10 tablespoons rum (optional)
60 marshmallows	1 cup heavy whipping cream
1/2 cup milk	Chocolate syrup to taste
3 cups heavy whipping cream	1/4 cup sliced almonds, toasted

Line the side and bottom of a 10-inch springform pan with ladyfingers. Combine the marshmallows and milk in the top of a double boiler. Place over simmering water. Cook until melted and smooth, stirring frequently. Let cool slightly. Beat 3 cups whipping cream in a mixing bowl until peaks form. Fold in the rum. Fold in the marshmallow mixture. Beat 1 cup whipping cream in a mixing bowl until peaks form. Add the chocolate syrup gradually, mixing constantly at low speed until combined. Fold into the marshmallow mixture. Do not overmix; the mixture should appear marbled. Spoon into the springform pan. Sprinkle with the almonds. Chill, covered, until serving time. Drizzle with additional chocolate syrup just before serving. This dessert freezes well. Thaw in the refrigerator before serving.

SERVES 8 TO 10

Amaretto Cheese Pie

This recipe was submitted by the Junior Auxiliary of McMinnville, Tennessee. The JA of McMinnville mentors teens at a teen club in the community through the LIGHTHOUSE project.

CRUST
1 1/2 cups finely crushed
   chocolate wafers
1 cup blanched almonds, crushed
1/3 cup sugar
1/2 cup (1 stick) butter, melted

FILLING
8 ounces cream cheese, softened
1 cup sugar

3 egg yolks
1 tablespoon amaretto
1 cup heavy whipping cream
3 egg whites
1 (4-ounce) package blanched
   sliced almonds
1 tablespoon butter
Amaretto

To prepare the crust, mix the chocolate wafers, almonds, sugar and butter in a bowl. Press over the bottom and up the side of two greased glass pie plates.

To prepare the filling, beat the cream cheese and sugar in a mixing bowl until light and fluffy. Add the egg yolks and amaretto. Beat until combined. Beat the whipping cream in a mixing bowl until firm peaks form. Fold into the creamed mixture. Beat the egg whites in a mixing bowl until stiff peaks form. Fold into the creamed mixture. Pour into the pie shells. Freeze, covered, until firm. Toast the almonds in the butter in a skillet; drain. Sprinkle over the pie just before serving. Slice the pie and place on dessert plates. Drizzle each slice with 1 tablespoon amaretto.

SERVES 12 TO 16

Weidman's Black Bottom Pie

The Junior Auxiliary of Meridian, Mississippi, contributed this recipe. The JA of Meridian is a charter chapter of NAJA, a member since 1941.

"Several years ago while browsing in a bookstore, I picked up a JA cookbook to read. I discovered not only the flavor of good foods but also the good works of Junior Auxiliary. Intrigued, I contacted NAJA headquarters and asked for more information. I shared this information with friends and quickly discovered we really wanted to belong to this organization. Truly the quest for good food led to good works for our community."

—CHARTER MEMBER, JA OF MADISON COUNTY

14 gingersnaps, finely crushed
5 tablespoons butter, melted
4 egg yolks, beaten
2 cups milk, scalded
1/2 cup sugar
1 1/2 tablespoons cornstarch
1 1/2 ounces unsweetened
  chocolate, melted
1 teaspoon vanilla extract

1 envelope unflavored gelatin
2 tablespoons cold water
2 tablespoons bourbon
4 egg whites
1/4 teaspoon cream of tartar
1/2 cup sugar
Sweetened whipped cream
Unsweetened chocolate shavings

Mix the gingersnaps and butter in a bowl. Press over the bottom of a 9-inch deep-dish pie plate. Bake at 325 degrees for 10 minutes. Let stand until cool.

Temper the egg yolks by adding a small portion of the milk to the egg yolks in a bowl and whisking vigorously until combined. Whisk into the remaining milk. Place in the top of a double boiler over simmering water over medium heat. Mix 1/2 cup sugar and the cornstarch in a bowl. Stir into the milk mixture. Cook for 20 minutes or until the mixture coats the back of a spoon, stirring frequently. Mix 1 cup of the custard mixture with the melted chocolate in a bowl. Stir in the vanilla and pour into the pie shell. Chill until cold.

Sprinkle the gelatin over the cold water in a medium bowl. Let stand for 2 to 3 minutes to soften; mix well. Stir in the remaining custard mixture. Let stand until cool. Stir in the bourbon. Beat the egg whites and cream of tartar in a mixing bowl until foamy. Add 1/2 cup sugar gradually, beating constantly until combined. Beat until stiff peaks form. Fold into the custard mixture and spoon over the chocolate layer. Chill until firm. Top with whipped cream and sprinkle with chocolate shavings.

SERVES 6 TO 8

Chocolate Italian Cream Cake

CAKE
5 egg whites
1/2 cup (1 stick) butter, softened
1/2 cup shortening
2 cups sugar
5 egg yolks
2 1/4 cups all-purpose flour
1/4 cup unsweetened baking cocoa
1 teaspoon baking soda
1 cup buttermilk
1 cup sweetened flaked coconut
2/3 cup finely chopped pecans
2 teaspoons vanilla extract

CHOCOLATE CREAM CHEESE FROSTING
12 ounces cream cheese, softened
3/4 cup (1 1/2 sticks) butter, softened
2 1/2 teaspoons vanilla extract
1/2 teaspoon cinnamon
1 1/2 (1-pound) packages confectioners' sugar
3/4 cup baking cocoa
1/2 cup buttermilk

To prepare the cake, beat the egg whites in a mixing bowl until stiff peaks form; set aside. Beat the butter and shortening in a mixing bowl until smooth and creamy. Add the sugar gradually, beating constantly until combined. Cream until light and fluffy. Add the egg yolks one at a time, mixing well after each addition. Combine the flour, baking cocoa and baking soda. Add the dry ingredients and the buttermilk alternately to the creamed mixture, beginning and ending with the dry ingredients and mixing well at low speed after each addition. Stir in the coconut, pecans and vanilla. Fold in the egg whites. Spoon into three greased and floured 8-inch cake pans.

Bake at 325 degrees for 25 to 30 minutes or until a wooden pick inserted in the center comes out clean. Cool in the pans for 10 minutes. Remove to a wire rack to cool completely.

To prepare the frosting, beat the cream cheese, butter, vanilla and cinnamon at medium speed in a mixing bowl until smooth and creamy. Mix the confectioners' sugar and baking cocoa in a bowl. Add to the cream cheese mixture alternately with the buttermilk, beginning and ending with the confectioners' sugar mixture and mixing well at low speed after each addition. Spread between the layers and over the top and side of the cooled cake.

SERVES 10 TO 12

Kahlúa Cake

THE DINAH, *the cookbook of the Junior Auxiliary of McComb, Mississippi, contains this recipe. The JA of McComb is a charter chapter of NAJA, a member since 1941.*

AWARD WINNER:

FILLING THE GAP—

JA OF OSCEOLA

No family. No home. No money. That was the plight of our local scholarship recipient winner for 2005. An excellent student with the possibility of a bright future, but no family or finances to support him. Osceola "filled the gap" to send him toward a brighter future.

1 (2-layer) package yellow cake mix
1 (4-ounce) package chocolate instant pudding mix
4 eggs
1 cup vegetable oil
1/2 cup granulated sugar

1/3 cup Kahlúa
1/3 cup vodka
3/4 cup water
1/4 cup Kahlúa
1/2 cup confectioners' sugar

Mix the cake mix, pudding mix, eggs, oil, granulated sugar, 1/3 cup Kahlúa, the vodka and water in a bowl until smooth. The batter will be runny. Pour into a bundt pan. Bake at 350 degrees for 40 minutes. Let stand until cool. Invert the cake onto a wire rack. Mix 1/4 cup Kahlúa and the confectioners' sugar in a bowl until smooth. Pour the glaze over the cooled cake.

SERVES 16

Peanut Butter Chip Brownies

The Junior Auxiliary of Osceola, Arkansas, selected this recipe for this collection. The JA of Osceola won the 2006 Louise Eskrigge Crump Award for FILLING THE GAP, *a project to provide support to a college student in need.*

1 cup (2 sticks) butter, softened
3 ounces cream cheese, softened
2 cups sugar
3 eggs
1 teaspoon vanilla extract
1 cup all-purpose flour

3/4 cup baking cocoa
1/2 teaspoon salt
1/2 teaspoon baking powder
1 cup (6 ounces) peanut butter chips

Beat the butter, cream cheese and sugar at medium speed in a mixing bowl for 2 minutes. Scrape the side of the bowl and beat for 1 minute or until light and fluffy. Add the eggs and vanilla. Beat for 2 minutes. Combine the flour, baking cocoa, salt and baking powder. Add to the creamed mixture gradually, beating constantly at low speed until combined. Beat for 2 minutes. Stir in the peanut butter chips. Spoon into a 9×13-inch baking dish sprayed with nonstick cooking spray. Bake at 325 degrees for 35 to 40 minutes.

MAKES 2 DOZEN

Cappuccino-Frosted Brownies

BROWNIES

4 ounces unsweetened
  baking chocolate

2 cups sugar

3/4 cup (1 1/2 sticks) butter, chopped

4 eggs

1 cup all-purpose flour

1 teaspoon vanilla extract

1 cup (6 ounces) semisweet
  chocolate chips

**CAPPUCCINO BUTTERCREAM
  FROSTING**

1 envelope instant mocha
  cappuccino mix

1/4 cup hot milk

1/2 cup (1 stick) butter, softened

1 (1-pound) package
  confectioners' sugar

To prepare the brownies, combine the chocolate, sugar and butter in a large microwave-safe bowl. Microwave on High for 1 1/2 minutes or until melted and smooth, stirring after 1 minute and then stirring after 30 seconds until smooth. Add the eggs one at a time, mixing well after each addition. Stir in the flour and vanilla. Stir in the chocolate chips. Pour into a lightly greased 9×13-inch baking pan. Bake at 350 degrees for 30 to 35 minutes or until a wooden pick inserted in the center comes out clean. Cool on a wire rack.

To prepare the frosting, dissolve the cappuccino mix in the hot milk in a small cup or bowl; let stand until cool. Mix the cappuccino and butter at medium speed in a mixing bowl until smooth. Add the confectioners' sugar gradually, beating constantly until smooth and fluffy. Spread over the cooled brownies. Garnish with chocolate shavings. Cut into squares.

MAKES 2 DOZEN

Chocolate Biscuits

The Junior Auxiliary of Lewisburg, Tennessee, donated this favorite recipe. The JA of Lewisburg distributes coats to needy families with the KEEP OUR CHILDREN WARM *project.*

1 (8-count) can refrigerator biscuits

16 chocolate candy kisses

1/4 cup (1/2 stick) butter, melted

1 cup confectioners' sugar

Cut each portion of biscuit dough into halves. Wrap each half around a chocolate candy kiss, covering the kiss completely and sealing all edges and holes in the dough. Bake according to the package directions until golden brown. Dip in the butter and roll in the confectioners' sugar.

MAKES 16

Chocolate Chip Cookies

1 cup (2 sticks) butter, softened
1 cup packed brown sugar
1/2 cup granulated sugar
1 teaspoon vanilla extract
2 eggs, beaten
2 3/4 cups all-purpose flour

1 teaspoon baking soda
1 teaspoon salt
4 cups (24 ounces) milk
   chocolate chips
1/2 cup chopped walnuts

Cream the butter, brown sugar, granulated sugar and vanilla in a mixing bowl until light and fluffy. Beat in the eggs. Combine the flour, baking soda and salt. Add to the creamed mixture and beat until combined. Stir in the chocolate chips and walnuts. Drop by rounded teaspoonfuls onto a cookie sheet. Bake at 375 degrees for 8 to 10 minutes.

MAKES 3 DOZEN

Creamy Kahlúa Fudge

This recipe is from the Junior Auxiliary of Hattiesburg, Mississippi. The JA of Hattiesburg won the 2005–2006 Presidents Award following the chapter's recovery efforts from Hurricane Katrina.

1 1/3 cups sugar
1 (7-ounce) jar marshmallow creme
2/3 cup evaporated milk
1/4 cup (1/2 stick) butter
1/4 cup Kahlúa
1/4 teaspoon salt

2 cups (12 ounces) semisweet
   chocolate chips
1 cup (6 ounces) milk
   chocolate chips
2/3 cup chopped pecans or almonds
1 teaspoon vanilla extract

Combine the sugar, marshmallow creme, evaporated milk, butter, Kahlúa and salt in a 2-quart saucepan. Bring to a rapid boil, stirring frequently. Boil for 5 minutes, stirring constantly. Remove from the heat and add the semisweet chocolate chips and milk chocolate chips. Stir until melted and smooth. Stir in the pecans and vanilla. Pour into a foil-lined 8×8-inch baking pan. Chill, covered, until firm. Cut into squares.

MAKES 2 3/4 POUNDS

AWARD WINNER:
SOUTH MISSISSIPPI
CHILDREN'S CENTER—
JA OF HATTIESBURG
In 1982, the Junior Auxiliary of Hattiesburg identified the need for a shelter to house teenage girls who were without a safe place to stay. These girls, who were removed from their homes due to abuse or neglect, had been previously housed at a detention center due to a lack of foster homes or alternative placement. JA of Hattiesburg took on the monumental task of founding, developing, and managing the Hattiesburg Emergency Girls Shelter.

Junior Auxiliary Prayer

Send us, O God, as Thy messengers to the hearts without a home, to lives without love, to the crowds without a guide. Send us to the children whom none have blessed, to the famished whom none have visited, to the fallen whom none have lifted, to the bereaved whom none have comforted.

Kindle Thy flame on the altars of our hearts, that others may be warmed thereby; cause Thy light to shine in our souls, that others may see the way; keep our sympathies and insight ready, our wills keen, our hands quick to help others in their need.

Grant us clear vision, true judgment, with great daring as we seek to right the wrong; and so endow us with cheerful love that we may minister to the suffering and forlorn even as Thou wouldst. May the blessing of God Almighty, the Father, the Son, and the Holy Spirit, rest upon us and upon all our work. May He give us light to guide us, courage to support us, and love to unite us now and forever more. Amen.

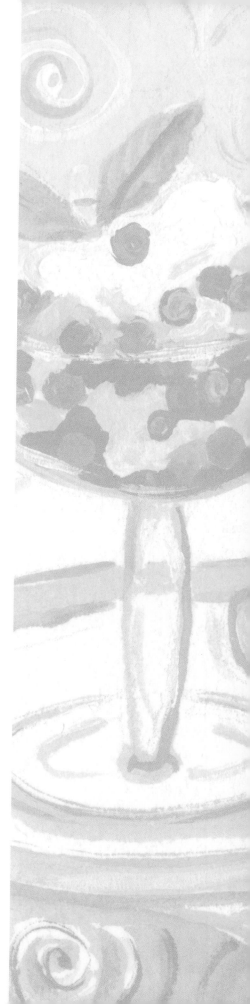

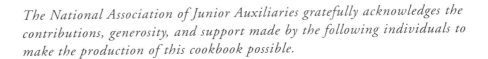

Donors

The National Association of Junior Auxiliaries gratefully acknowledges the contributions, generosity, and support made by the following individuals to make the production of this cookbook possible.

Silver Spoons
Blueberry Afternoons

Cookbook Committee

Co-Chairs
Esther N. Herring
and
Lyn I. Patrick

Copy Editor
Lyn Walker

Recipe Selection
Ruth McCauley
and
Brandi Provias

Publicity
Kelly Chaney
and
Amanda Fontaine

NAJA Executive Director
Merrill Greenlee

NAJA 2007–2008 President
Vickie Tidwell

Mary Carole Bowers,
NAJA Foundation Chair, 2007–08

Lois Boykin,
NAJA President, 2001–02

Margaret Brooks,
NAJA President, 1985–86

Mandy Buchanan,
*Active Member,
JA of Laurel, MS*

Carol Caruso,
NAJA President, 2006–07

Kelly Chaney,
NAJA Public Relations Chair, 2007–08

Jodi Clark,
Region VI Director

Suzanna Johnson Clark,
NAJA President, 2002–03

Jean Kellems Elmore,
NAJA President, 1989–90

Cara Evans,
*Active Member,
JA of Marion, AR*

Dolores Fratesi,
*Chapter Development Coordinator,
1998–2005*

Amanda Fontaine,
*NAJA Marketing Vice President,
2007–08*

LuAnne B. Givens,
NAJA President, 1991–92

Merrill Greenlee,
NAJA Executive Director

Ann Guice,
NAJA President, 1981–82

Sara Francis Hardy,
Active Member, JA of Oxford, MS

Michelle Heidelberg,
NAJA President, 1998–99

Esther N. Herring,
NAJA First Vice-President, 2007–08

Angela Hinton,
Active Member, JA of Oxford, MS

Beth Holbert,
NAJA Treasurer, 2007–08

Sharon Hudson,
Chapter Advisor, 2007–08

Carmen Jabour,
Chapter Support Coordinator

Ellen Ann Johnson,
NAJA Galleria Director

Beverly Jones,
NAJA President, 1986–87

Wendy Jones,
Chapter Support Coordinator

Christy Keirn,
NAJA Second Vice President, 2007–08

Amanda Knauer,
NAJA Third Vice President, 2007–08

Karen Knight,
Active Member, JA of Cabot, AR

Ruth McCauley,
NAJA Education Committee

B. J. Nichols,
NAJA Resource Center Coordinator

Leia O'Fallon,
Active Member, JA of Monticello, AR

Jeresa Parten,
Associate Member, JA of Jonesboro, AR

Lyn I. Patrick,
NAJA President, 2005–06

Cindy Paul,
Associate Member, JA of Jonesboro, AR

Vicki Pentecost,
NAJA President, 2003–04

Amy Pinkston,
Chapter Support Coordinator

Brandi Provias,
Region IV Director

Cindy Odom Rice,
NAJA President, 1994–95

Mary Anne Roscopf,
NAJA President, 1964–65

Norma Delong Richards,
*NAJA Executive Director,
1984–2000*

Cindy Rood,
NAJA President, 1984–85

Mary Aleese Schreiber,
*NAJA President,
1983–84*

Eleanor Slaughter,
NAJA President, 1956–57

Linda Lee Smith,
NAJA Crownlet Editor

Elaine Darras Swetland,
NAJA President, 1975–76

Lynda Terney,
NAJA President, 1978–79

Vickie Tidwell,
NAJA President, 2007–08

Johnnie Tolleson,
Education Committee Chair, 2007–08

Robin Townsend,
NAJA President, 1995–96

Jacquie Turner,
NAJA President, 1968–69

Johnna Walker,
Region I Director

Lyn Walker,
NAJA Recording Secretary, 2007–08

Ann Elise Walston,
NAJA Membership Secretary

Wilma Wilbanks,
NAJA President, 1987–88

Joyce Wyatt,
NAJA President, 1962–63

Index

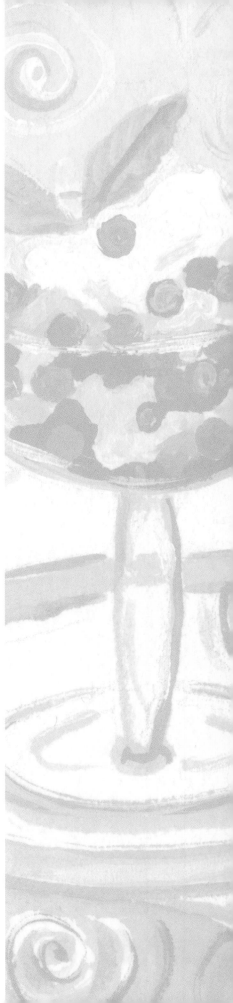

Silver Spoons
Blueberry Afternoons

A Crowning Collection of Recipes and Memories from
the National Association of Junior Auxiliaries, Inc.

National Association of Junior Auxiliaries, Inc.
P. O. Box 1873
Greenville, MS 38702-1873
www.najanet.org
Telephone: 662-332-3000
FAX: 662-332-3076

Name_____

Street Address_____

City_____ State_____Zip_____

Telephone_____

YOUR ORDER	QUANTITY	TOTAL
Silver Spoons, Blueberry Afternoons ($24.95)	_____	$_____
MS residents add $1.75 per book for sales tax		$_____
Shipping and handling, $6 for first book, $3 for each additional copy to the same address		$_____
TOTAL		$_____

Method of Payment: ❏ MasterCard ❏ Visa

❏ Check made payable to NAJA

Credit Card Number_____ Expiration Date_____

Signature_____

Photocopies accepted.

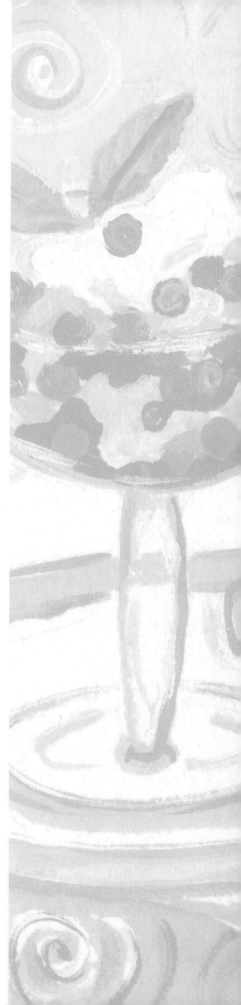